THE CHANGELING

The Mathew Carey Library
of English and American Literature

Department of English
University of Pennsylvania

THE MATHEW CAREY LIBRARY

Like the early Philadelphia publisher after whom this series is named, the Mathew Carey Library aims to publish good but inexpensive editions of English and American texts which are worthy of reading and study but which are not otherwise readily available.

Titles are selected for literary value, special interest of a particular edition, or relevance to literary history, rather than merely for rarity.

Because emphasis is placed on providing an authentic text for both scholarly and classroom use, notes and other editorial apparatus are held to a minimum.

Each volume is edited by a specialist in the literature of its kind or period and by a member of the Editorial Committee of the Department of English of the University of Pennsylvania.

The Changeling

By THOMAS MIDDLETON and WILLIAM ROWLEY

Edited by Matthew W. Black

Philadelphia: University of Pennsylvania Press

7511
Printed in the United States of America

INTRODUCTION

The Changeling is a powerful psychological tragedy which has for theme the moral degeneration of a highborn Spanish girl, Beatrice-Joanna, through a crime prompted by obsessive love. A comic subplot concerns the antics of a young rake, Antonio, who contrives to have himself committed to an insane asylum for love of the physician-proprietor's handsome wife. This subplot has been criticized as "nauseous" and "better excised," but is in fact a burlesque contrasting treatment of the farcical effects of mad infatuation, i.e. of passionate love working upon a temperament less self-centered, humorless, and ruthless than that of Beatrice-Joanna. The presence in the main and subsidiary plots of a common theme; the interpenetration and ultimate combining of the two story-lines; the fact that although Antonio, who goes from sanity to pretended lunacy to sanity once again, is the "changeling" referred to in the title, practically all of the principal characters also change; and the tolerance of the seventeenth-century audience toward the mingling of tragedy and farce—all these considerations help a modern reader to accept the whole as possessing a certain artistic unity.

In his copy of the first quarto edition of the play, the eighteenth-century scholar Edmond Malone, who apparently had access to portions of the records of the Master of the Revels which are now lost, wrote that it was "licensed to be acted by the Lady Elizabeth's Servants at the Phoenix, May 7, 1622." Since

51815

the two principal sources of the play were entered for publication in the *Stationers' Register* on June 7, 1621, and March 11, 1622, respectively, we conclude that *The Changeling* was composed during the winter and spring of 1622. It was written in collaboration by Thomas Middleton (1580–1627), otherwise notable for his realistic comedies of London life, and William Rowley (c.1585–1626), an actor famous for robust comic roles and—perhaps for this reason—much in demand as a collaborator. Middleton was probably responsible for the bulk of the tragic plot, with its fine climax in Act III, scene iv, Rowley for the comic subplot, the opening, and the final scenes. But traces of both authors are found in every scene, so that it is likely that by their diverse gifts they not only influenced but inspired each other. Certainly Middleton in tragedy never surpassed his achievement here, and his subtler psychology, smoother versification, and mastery of dramatic irony—a quality which pervades the piece to a remarkable degree—must have spurred on Rowley's cruder, more virile genius to the fine denouement in V.iii. 149–161, a memorable passage of dramatic poetry.

The stage history of *The Changeling* indicates a somewhat greater than average popularity during the last two decades before the closing of the theaters in 1642 and for a few years just before and after the Restoration in 1660. Contemporary references to Antonio, the changeling, suggest that this part was a favorite.[1] A performance at the court at Whitehall on January 4, 1624 is on record.[2] The performances "at the Privat house in Drury-Lane, and Salisbury Court" mentioned on the title page of the quarto of 1653 most likely took place before 1636, when Queen Henrietta's company, which succeeded the Lady Elizabeth's men at the Phoenix and presumably took over the play, foundered.[3] *The Changeling* is one of the plays that the Lord Chamberlain,

[1] These are collected by N. W. Bawcutt in his edition of the play in the Revels series (1958), pp. xxvi–xxviii.
[2] J. Q. Adams, *The Dramatic Records of Sir Henry Herbert* (1917), p. 51.
[3] G. E. Bentley, *The Jacobean and Caroline Stage,* I (1941). 219.

on August 10, 1639, protected for William Beeston, the manager of a boy company.[4] In 1659 it was revived at the Phoenix by a company organized by John Rhodes.[5] When this troupe became the Duke's Company under the management of Sir William Davenant, it gave further performances of the play, one of which, on February 23, 1661, was seen by Samuel Pepys.[6] Performances by the same company at "the Theatre in Lincolns-Inn Fields" are mentioned on the title page of the quarto of 1668. The performance at court on November 30, 1668 is the last on record before the twentieth century.[7] Since 1930 there have been several revivals by amateur and semi-professional players. Late in October 1964 thirty-eight performances were scheduled by the Repertory Company of the Lincoln Center, New York.

The first record of the play in print is an entry in the Stationers' Register on 19 October 1652: "M^r. Mosely. Entred . . . a Comedie called y^e Changeling. written by Rowley" (Greg, *Bibliography*, i. 60). The first quarto (Greg, no. 712, AI†) duly appeared in the next year:

THE | CHANGELING: | As it was Acted (with great Applause) | at the Privat house in DRURY-LANE, | and *Salisbury Court*. || Written by $\left\{ \begin{array}{c} THOMAS\ MIDLETON, \\ and \\ WILLIAM\ ROWLEY. \end{array} \right\}$ Gent'. ||

Never Printed before. || *LONDON,* | Printed for HUMPHREY MOSELEY, and are to | be sold at his shop at the sign of the *Princes-Arms* | in St *Pauls* Church-yard, 1653.

Collation: [A1] B–I^4 (–I4). Greg also lists a variant imprint (AI*)—"*LONDON,* | Printed in the Year, 1653."—omitting Moseley's name and the location of his shop, and surmises that, since the issues are identical in all but the title page, this may

---

[4] Malone Society *Collections*, vol. II, part III (1931), pp. 389–390.
[5] John Downes, *Roscius Anglicanus*, ed. Montague Summers [c. 1929], pp. 17–19.
[6] *The Diary of Samuel Pepys*, ed. H. B. Wheatley (1899), I. 351.
[7] William Van Lennep, "Plays on the English Stage 1669–1672," *Theatre Notebook* XVI (1961), p. 13.

have been intended for private circulation. Rollins thinks that the publication may have been delayed by Puritan prohibition which, in 1653, extended even to the printing of plays, and that the omission of Moseley's name and place of business suggests that he may have wished to avoid trouble with the authorities.[8] C. W. Miller (*Studies in Bibliography* iii [1950–1951], 164) identifies the large ornament on B1^r as one of those used by Thomas Newcomb, who was presumably the printer. It has been suggested that the long interval between production and publication had given rise to some inexpert cutting of scenes, as for example at IV.iii.145 ff., where a beating is led up to, then tamely avoided, but the evidence for this is unimpressive.

A reissue (Greg, AII) appeared fifteen years later with a cancel title page:

THE | CHANGELING: | As it was Acted (with great | Applause) by the Servants of His | Royal Highness the Duke of *York,* at | the Theatre in *Lincolns-Inn* Fields. || [ornament] || *LONDON,* | Printed for *A.M.* and sold by | *Thomas Dring,* at the *White Lyon,* over against | the Inner *Temple-Gate* in *Fleet-street.* 1668. || Where you may be Furnish'd with | most sorts of *Plays.*

On A1^v appear a reprint of the "Drammatis Personae" and a publisher's advertisement, probably Dring's.

My collation of the University of Pennsylvania copy (Greg AI†) with the Huntington copy, and collations by Lawrence [9] and Bawcutt [10] of the Huntington with the British Museum and Bodleian copies show press corrections in the outer formes of gatherings B and D, but only two substantive corrections: D1^r *w'are* for *we are* (II.i.151) improves the meter (the contraction is used frequently elsewhere in the play) and D3^r *myself of that* for *myself that* (II.ii.131) improves both meter and sense. As Bawcutt (p.xvi) observes, the presence of uncorrected sheets in

---

[8] H. E. Rollins, "A Contribution to the History of the English Commonwealth Drama," *S. P.* xviii (1921), 267–333.

[9] R. G. Lawrence, *The Changeling,* University of Wisconsin Dissertation, 1956.

[10] *Op. cit.,* p. xvi.

the reissue of 1668 indicates that the play was printed only once. Both Lawrence and Bawcutt consider that the clear marking of entrances and exits and the occurrence of imperative stage directions (cf. III.iii.89, V.i.11, 73.1) suggest a theatrical prompt copy as the source of the text.

The Changeling has been included in most of the collections of the old drama, the earliest modern edition being that of C. W. Dilke, *Old English Plays,* 1815, IV, 219–324, and in editions of Middleton by Dyce (1840) and Bullen (1885); it has been edited separately by Lawrence, Bawcutt, and the present editor.

The present text is that of the (corrected) copy of the quarto in the library of the University of Pennsylvania with the following exceptions:

1. The spelling has been modernized. I have followed the Q spelling of non-syllabic -*ed,* '*d,* and -*red,* but have marked syllabic -*ed* and the word *perfect* (V.iii.115), which may be an adjective, but which I take to be a truncated past participle, with a grave accent (-*èd, perfèct*). Spellings with -*th*- for -*d*- or the reverse are modernized (*murder, burden, fathoms*). Quarto contractions such as *Y'are, I've,* expanded by some editors for the sake of the meter, are retained. Proper names are given in the current form (*Valencia* rather than *Valentia*).

2. Like all other editors, I print the text, so far as possible, as normal lines of blank verse. The quarto is badly "mislined" and therefore open to considerable rectification. Most of the necessary adjustments were made by Dilke and Dyce. With four exceptions, my lineation and numbering are those of Bawcutt's Revels edition, including the excellent system of numbering stage directions which occupy separate lines by adding a decimal to the number of the preceding line of dialogue. At II.i.125, IV.ii.60, and V.iii.181, however, I allow an exclamatory syllable (*So, Sir, O*) to stand as a separate line on the analogy of *Ha!* at V.ii.61, so as to normalize the rest of the three lines as iambic pentameter. At II.i.139 I retain *in his passions,* which most editors omit, and make *And how dangerous* a separate two- or three-beat line, scan-

ning *Aňd hŏw dángĕróus* or *Aňd hŏw dángĕróus,* on the analogy
of I.i.235, II.ii.82, III.iv.57, 161, IV.i.156, and V.ii.42, not to
mention a dozen possibly metrical short lines in the subplot. Line
II.i.140 is thus preceded and followed by a normal blank verse,
and the retained phrase enriches rather than damages the sense
(see the note).

Moreover, the practice of the authors is not entirely uniform.
In many lines, for example, the caesura seems to supply an un-
accented tenth syllable; cf. I.i.108, *You seem'd displeas'd Lady
on the sudden.* Occasional lines of only four beats occur; others
of eleven or twelve syllables are so rough that they might be taken
as prose were it not that many of them are spoken by upper-class
persons and that the distinction of verse for these and prose for
persons of less consequence, such as Lollio and the castle servants,
seems to be rather carefully observed.

3. In order to assist the reader in visualizing the action, I have
divided the acts into scenes, amplified the stage directions and
added new ones, and marked asides; these additions are enclosed
in square brackets. I have, however, succumbed to the tempta-
tion to retain imperative stage directions, with their suggestion of
the busy, anxious prompter in the wings. Many but not all of the
asides were marked by Dilke and Dyce; that at III.iv.89 was
added by Oliphant (1929), that at I.i.171 by Brooke and Paradise
(1933), those at I.i.50, 56, II.i.68, and IV.i.100 by Bawcutt, and
those at IV.i.89, IV.ii.35, and V.iii.104 by the present editor.
The dash, in addition to its usual function of marking an inter-
ruption of thought and/or syntax within a sentence, is used to
signal the end of an aside and any significant change within a
speech, in the person addressed, in the subject under discussion,
or in the speaker's tone of voice.

4. I have not emulated the quixotic attempts to follow the
quarto punctuation. As Lawrence shows, the work of Newcomb's
shop on this play is generally careless. The punctuation is merely
erratic. The presence of dozens of errors such as the omission of
any mark at the end of a speech, the insertion of a colon or period
after a portion of a sentence which then continues, the mechani-

cal marking of the caesura with a comma, make me suspect that other points are similarly untrustworthy. I have therefore used my own judgment as to the author's probable intention and punctuated accordingly. In other words, I have tried to make the text as easy as possible for the present-day reader to understand, by inserting or omitting points, but especially by substituting heavier ones in accordance with present-day usage.

5. Obvious misprints such as *aud* for *and* are corrected silently. All other alterations of the text of the quarto besides those summarized above are specified in an appendix (p. 141).

The notes are as full as space will allow. I have, however, refrained from glossing many unfamiliar terms (*basilisk, magnifico, pillory*) and classical allusions (*Esculapius, Bucephalus*) which are to be found in any good desk dictionary.

THE
CHANGELING:

As it was Acted (with great Applause)
at the Privat house in D R U R Y $ L A N E,
and *Salisbury Court.*

Written by { *THOMAS MIDLETON,* and *WILLIAM ROWLEY.* } Gent°.

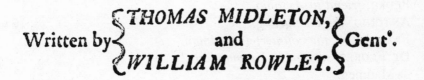

Never Printed before.

LONDON,

Printed for H U M P H R E Y M O S E L E Y, and are to
be sold at his shop at the sign of the *Princes-Arms*
in St *Pauls* Church-yard, 1 6 5 3.

Dramatis Personae

VERMANDERO, *father to Beatrice [governor of the castle of Alicante.]*

TOMAZO DE PIRACQUO, *a noble lord.*

ALONZO DE PIRACQUO, *his brother, suitor to Beatrice.*

ALSEMERO, *a nobleman, afterwards married to Beatrice.*   5

JASPERINO, *his friend.*

ALIBIUS, *a jealous doctor.*

LOLLIO, *his man.*

PEDRO, *friend to Antonio.*

ANTONIO, *the changeling.*   10

FRANCISCUS, *the counterfeit madman.*

DE FLORES, *servant to Vermandero.*

  Madmen.

  Servants.

BEATRICE [-JOANNA], *daughter to Vermandero.*   15

DIAPHANTA, *her waiting woman.*

ISABELLA, *wife to Alibius.*

               The Scene: *Alicante.*

ANTONIO, the changeling] A changeling may be not only "one who is changed" but also a half-wit or idiot such as Antonio prentends to be. *OED* gives the earliest example of the latter meaning as 1642, but "changeling" is so explained in Scot's *Discovery of Witchcraft* (1584).

Alicante] A seaport on the east coast of Spain, about seventy-five miles due south of Valencia.

ACTUS PRIMUS

Enter ALSEMERO.

Als.
'Twas in the temple where I first beheld her,
And now again the same. What omen yet
Follows of that? None but imaginary?
Why should my hopes of fate be timorous?
The place is holy, so is my intent: 5
I love her beauties to the holy purpose,
And that, methinks, admits comparison
With man's first creation, the place blest,
And is his right home back, if he achieve it.
The church hath first begun our interview   10

I.i.] Q marks act divisions only. Scene i takes place "Near the Harbor of Alicante."

2–3. *now . . . same*] In the source Alsemero and Beatrice meet in a church and fall in love during their prayers. Presumably he has just seen her there again.

6. *the holy purpose*] Marriage.

7–9.] Marriage may be likened to Paradise or Eden, man's true home lost by Adam's fall. To it Alsemero and his bride may return.

And that's the place must join us into one;
So there's beginning and perfection too.
                    Enter JASPERINO.

Jas.

O, sir, are you here? Come, the wind's fair with you;
Y'are like to have a swift and pleasant passage.

Als.

Sure y'are deceived, friend; 'tis contrary   15
In my best judgment.

Jas.   What, for Malta?
If you could buy a gale amongst the witches,
They could not serve you such a lucky pennyworth
As comes a God's name.

Als.   Even now I observ'd
The temple's vane to turn full in my face;   20
I know 'tis against me.

Jas.   Against you?
Then you know not where you are.

Als.   Not well, indeed.

Jas.

Are you not well, sir?

Als.   Yes, Jasperino,
Unless there be some hidden malady
Within me that I understand not.

Jas.   And that   25
I begin to doubt, sir: I never knew
Your inclinations to travels at a pause,
With any cause to hinder it, till now.

17.] Witches were reputed to control the winds; cf. *Macbeth*
I.iii.11.

18. *pennyworth*] Bargain.

19. *a*] In; "a God's name," in the course of nature.

26. *doubt*] Fear.

28. *With . . . it*] No matter what arose to hinder your inclina-
tion. Cf. II.i.84–5.

Ashore you were wont to call your servants up
And help to trap your horses for the speed;   30
At sea I have seen you weigh the anchor with 'em,
Hoist sails for fear to lose the foremost breath,
Be in continual prayers for fair winds;
And have you chang'd your orisons?

Als.   No, friend,
I keep the same church, same devotion.   35

Jas.

Lover I'm sure y'are none; the stoic was
Found in you long ago. Your mother nor
Best friends, who have set snares of beauty—ay,
And choice ones, too—could never trap you that way.
What might be the cause?

Als.   Lord, how violent   40
Thou art! I was but meditating of
Somewhat I heard within the temple.

Jas.

Is this violence? 'Tis but idleness
Compar'd with your haste yesterday.

Als.

I'm all this while a-going, man.   45

Enter Servants.

Jas.

Backwards, I think, sir. Look, your servants.

1 Ser.

The seamen call; shall we board your trunks?

Als.

No, not today.

30.] Help to harness the horses so as to get started the sooner.
31. *weigh . . . 'em*] Help the crew haul anchor.
34. *orisons*] Prayers.
36. *stoic*] Man free from passion.
47. *board*] Stow aboard.

Jas.

'Tis the critical day, it seems—and the sign in
Aquarius!

2 Ser.   [*aside.*]

We must not to sea today! This smoke will   50
bring forth fire.

Als.

Keep all on shore; I do not know the end—
Which needs I must do—of an affair in hand
Ere I can go to sea.

1 Ser.

Well, your pleasure.   55

2 Ser.   [*aside.*]

Let him e'en take his leisure, too; we are
    safer on land.   *Exeunt Servants.*

Enter BEATRICE, DIAPHANTA, *and Servants.* [ALSEMERO *greets*
        BEATRICE *and kisses her. They talk apart.*]

Jas.   [*aside.*]

How now! The laws of the Medes are chang'd sure.
Salute a woman! He kisses, too. Wonderful! Where learnt
he this? And does it perfectly, too. In my conscience, 60
he ne'er rehears'd it before. Nay, go on! This will be
stranger and better news at Valencia than if he had ran-
som'd half Greece from the Turk.

Bea.

You are a scholar, sir.

Als.   A weak one, lady.

Bea.

Which of the sciences is this love you speak of?   65

Als.

From your tongue I take it to be music.

---

49. *critical*] Astrologically decisive for good or ill.

    and . . . Aquarius] He fears to embark even though the
sign of the zodiac is the water-bearer!

60. *In my conscience*] Upon my soul.

63.] Greece was under Turkish rule 1460–1830.

Bea.

You are skilful in't, can sing at first sight.

Als.

And I have show'd you all my skill at once.
I want more words to express me further
And must be forc'd to repetition: 70
I love you dearly.

Bea.   Be better advis'd, sir:
Our eyes are sentinels unto our judgments
And should give certain judgment what they see;
But they are rash sometimes and tell us wonders
Of common things, which when our judgments find,   75
They can then check the eyes and call them blind.

Als.

But I am further, lady; yesterday
Was mine eyes' employment, and hither now
They brought my judgment, where are both agreed.
Both houses then consenting, 'tis agreed;   80
Only there wants the confirmation
By the hand royal: that's your part, lady.

Bea.

O, there's one above me, sir. [*Aside.*] For five days past
To be recall'd! Sure mine eyes were mistaken:
This was the man was meant me. That he should come   85
So near his time, and miss it!

---

69. *want*] Lack.

75. *Of*] About.

   which . . . find] For which errors, when our judgments discover them.

76. *check*] Rebuke.

77. *further*] Past that point.

78. *Was . . . employment*] I used my eyes.

80. *houses*] Commons and Lords, i.e. eyes and judgment.

83. *one*] Her father, who favors Alonzo's suit.

   five days past] The time when she became the betrothed of Alonzo.

Jas.   [*aside.*]
We might have come by the carriers from Valencia,
I see, and sav'd all our sea provision: we are at farthest,
sure. Methinks I should do something, too;
I meant to be a venturer in this voyage.   90
Yonder's another vessel; I'll board her;
If she be lawful prize, down goes her topsail.
                                    [*Greets* DIAPHANTA.]
                        Enter DE FLORES.

De F.
Lady, your father—
Bea.   Is in health, I hope.
De F.
Your eye shall instantly instruct you, lady.
He's coming hitherward.
Bea.   What needed, then,   95
Your duteous preface? I had rather
He had come unexpected. You must stall
A good presence with unnecessary blabbing;
And how welcome for your part you are
I'm sure you know.
De F.   [*aside.*]
Will't never mend, this scorn   100
One side nor other? Must I be enjoin'd

88–9. *we . . . sure*] It surely seems that this is the farthest we're
going.

90. *venturer*] One who shares the risk and the profit.

91. *vessel*] Diaphanta.
    board her] Accost her. Cf. *Twelfth Night* I.iii.60.

92. *down . . . topsail*] She'll surrender.

97. *stall*] Forestall (Dilke).

98. *a good presence*] The dignified appearance of my father.

100–1. *Will't . . . other*] Will she never cease to scorn me, or
I to expose myself to her scorn?

101. *enjoin'd*] Commanded (by my lust).

To follow still whilst she flies from me? Well,
Fates, do your worst! I'll please myself with sight
Of her at all opportunities,
If but to spite her anger; I know she had   105
Rather see me dead than living, and yet
She knows no cause for't but a peevish will.

Als.

You seem'd   displeas'd, lady, on the sudden.

Bea.

Your pardon, sir, 'tis my infirmity;
Nor can I other reason render you   110
Than his or hers, of some particular thing
They must abandon as a deadly poison,
Which to a thousand other tastes were wholesome;
Such to mine eyes is that same fellow there:
The same that report speaks of the basilisk.   115

Als.

This is a frequent frailty in our nature;
There's scarce a man amongst a thousand sound
But hath his imperfection: one distastes
The scent of roses, which to infinites
Most pleasing is and odoriferous;   120
One oil, the enemy of poison;
Another wine, the cheerer of the heart
And lively refresher of the countenance.
Indeed this fault—if so it be—is general:
There's scarce a thing but is both lov'd and loath'd;   125
Myself, I must confess, have the same frailty.

Bea.

And what may be your poison, sir? I am bold with you.

---

102. *still*] Always.
111. *his or hers*] Anyone else's reason.
117. *sound*] Normal, healthy people.
118. *distastes*] Dislikes.
119. *infinites*] Any number of people.

Als.

What might be your desire, perhaps: a cherry.

Bea.

I am no enemy to any creature
My memory has, but yon gentleman.   130

Als.

He does ill to tempt your sight, if he knew it.

Bea.

He cannot be ignorant of that, sir;
I have not spar'd to tell him so; and I want
To help myself, since he's a gentleman
In good respect with my father and follows him.   135

Als.

He's out of his place, then, now.

Jas.   [*They talk apart.*]

I am a mad wag, wench.

Dia.

So methinks; but for your comfort I can tell you we
have a doctor in the city that undertakes the cure of
such.

Jas.

Tush, I know what physic is best for the state of mine   140
own body.

Dia.

'Tis scarce a well-govern'd state, I believe.

Jas.

I could show thee such a thing with an ingredient that
we two would compound together, and if it did not tame
the maddest blood i' th' town for two hours after, I'll   145
ne'er profess physic again.

133–4. *want To*] Can't.
135. *In . . . with*] Well thought of by.
      follows him] Is one of his retainers.
139. *a doctor*] Alibius; see I.ii.
140. *physic*] Medicine.
146. *physic*] Medical science.

Dia.

A little poppy, sir, were good to cause you sleep.

Jas.

Poppy! I'll give thee a pop i' th' lips for that first, and
begin there. [*Kisses her.*] Poppy is one simple, indeed,
and cuckoo what-you-call't another. I'll discover no   150
more now; another time I'll show thee all.

Bea.

My father, sir.

         Enter VERMANDERO *and Servants.*

Ver.   O, Joanna, I came to meet thee.
Your devotion's ended?

Bea.   For this time, sir.
[*Aside.*] I shall change my saint, I fear me; I find   155
A giddy turning in me.—Sir, this while
I am beholding to this gentleman,
Who left his own way to keep me company,
And in discourse I find him much desirous
To see your castle. He hath deserv'd it, sir,   160
If ye please to grant it.

Ver.   With all my heart, sir.
Yet there's an article between: I must know
Your country. We use not to give survey
Of our chief strengths to strangers; our citadels
Are plac'd conspicuous to outward view   165
On promonts' tops, but within are secrets.

---

149. *simple*] Medicinal herb.

150. *cuckoo what-you-call't*] Cuckoo pintle-root, arum (Bawcutt).

      discover] Reveal.

155. *I . . . saint*] Change from religious to earthly devotion,
i.e. to Alsemero.

157. *beholding*] Indebted.

162. *article between*] Prior stipulation.

166. *promonts'*] Promontories'.

Als.

A Valencian, sir.

Ver.   A Valencian?

That's native, sir. Of what name, I beseech you?

Als.

Alsemero, sir.

Ver.   Alsemero! Not the son

Of John de Alsemero?

Als.   The same, sir.   170

Ver.

My best love bids you welcome.

Bea.   [*aside.*]

He was wont

To call me so, and then he speaks a most

Unfeigned truth.

Ver.   O, sir, I knew your father;

We two were in acquaintance long ago

Before our chins were worth Iulan down,   175

And so continued till the stamp of time

Had coin'd us into silver. Well, he's gone;

A good soldier went with him.

Als.

You went together in that, sir.

Ver.

No, by Saint Jaques, I came behind him;   180

Yet I have done somewhat, too. An unhappy day

Swallowed him at last at Gibraltar

In fight with those rebellious Hollanders;

Was it not so?

171–3. *He . . . truth*] My father was in the habit of calling me his "best love," and if he means that *I* bid you welcome, he speaks the real truth.

175. *were . . . down*] Had sprouted hair. *Iulan* refers to Iulus Ascanius, the adolescent son of Aeneas in the *Aeneid*.

180. *Saint Jaques*] St. James of Compostella, patron saint of Spain.

Als.   Whose death I had reveng'd,
  Or followed him in fate, had not the late league   185
  Prevented me.
Ver.   Ay, ay, 'twas time to breathe.—
  O, Joanna, I should ha' told thee news:
  I saw Piracquo lately.
Bea.   [*aside.*]
                                    That's ill news.
Ver.
  He's hot preparing for his day of triumph;
  Thou must be a bride within this sevennight.
Als.   [*aside.*]
                                    Ha!   190
Bea.
  Nay, good sir, be not so violent; with speed
  I cannot render satisfaction
  Unto the dear companion of my soul,
  Virginity, whom I thus long have liv'd with,
  And part with it so rude and suddenly.   195
  Can such friends divide, never to meet again,
  Without a solemn farewell?
Ver.   Tush, tush, there's a toy.
Als.   [*aside.*]
  I must now part, and never meet again
  With any joy on earth.—Sir, your pardon:
  My affairs call on me.
Ver.   How, sir? By no means;   200
  Not chang'd so soon, I hope. You must see my castle
  And her best entertainment ere we part;
  I shall think myself unkindly us'd, else.
  Come, come, let's on; I had good hope your stay

---

  185. *late league*] The Hague Armistice between Spain and the
Netherlands, 1609–1621.
  186. *Prevented me*] Anticipated my action.
  187. *breathe*] Rest from fighting, catch one's breath.
       toy] Whim.

Had been a while with us in Alicant;   205
I might have bid you to my daughter's wedding.
Als.   [*aside.*]
He means to feast me and poisons me beforehand!—
I should be dearly glad to be there, sir,
Did my occasions suit as I could wish.
Bea.
I shall be sorry if you be not there   210
When it is done, sir; but not so suddenly.
Ver.
I tell you, sir, the gentleman's complete,
A courtier and a gallant, enrich'd
With many fair and noble ornaments;
I would not change him for a son-in-law   215
For any he in Spain, the proudest he,
And we have great ones, that you know.
Als.   He's much
Bound to you, sir.
Ver.   He shall be bound to me
As fast as this tie can hold him; I'll want
My will else.
Bea.   [*aside.*]
                I shall want mine if you do it.   220
Ver.
But come; by the way I'll tell you more of him.
Als.   [*aside.*]
How shall I dare to venture in his castle
When he discharges murderers at the gate?

---

208. *dearly*] Very, very.

213. *courtier*] Three syllables.

218. *Bound . . . bound*] 1) Indebted; 2) united.

219–20. *want My will*] Lack what I desire. Beatrice echoes
her father's words.

221. *by the way*] As we go.

223. *murderers*] Small cannon. Alsemero means "He kills me
by talking of Beatrice's marriage to Alonzo."

But I must on, for back I cannot go.   224
Bea.   [*aside.*]
Not this serpent gone yet?   [*Drops a glove.*]
Ver.   Look, girl, thy glove's fall'n;
Stay, stay. De Flores, help a little.
[*Exeunt* VERMANDERO, ALSEMERO, JASPERINO, *and Servants.*]
De F.   Here, lady. [*Offers the glove.*]
Bea.
Mischief on your officious forwardness!
Who bade you stoop? They touch my hand no more:
There, for t'other's sake I part with this;
        [*Takes off the other glove and throws it down.*]
Take 'em and draw thine own skin off with 'em.   230
                Exeunt [BEATRICE *and* DIAPHANTA.]
De F.
Here's a favor come with a mischief! Now I know
She had rather wear my pelt tann'd in a pair
Of dancing pumps than I should thrust my fingers
Into her sockets here. I know she hates me
Yet cannot choose but love her. No matter: 235
If but to vex her, I'll haunt her still;
Though I get nothing else, I'll have my will.   *Exit.*

[I.ii]

                Enter ALIBIUS *and* LOLLIO.

Alib.
Lollio, I must trust thee with a secret;
But thou must keep it.

---

231. *favor*] A token, such as a lady's glove, worn by a knight
in a tournament.
        mischief] Ill wish. Cf. 230.
234. *sockets*] The fingers of her gloves.
I.ii.] A Room in Alibius' House.

Lol.

I was ever close to a secret, sir.

Alib.

The diligence that I have found in thee,
The care and industry already past   5
Assures me of thy good continuance.
Lollio, I have a wife.

Lol.

Fie, sir, 'tis too late to keep her a secret; she's
known to be married all the town and country over.

Alib.

Thou goest too fast, my Lollio. That knowledge,   10
I allow no man can be barr'd it;
But there is a knowledge which is nearer,
Deeper, and. sweeter, Lollio.

Lol.

Well, sir, let us handle that between you and I.

Alib.

'Tis that I go about, man. Lollio,   15
My wife is young.

Lol.

So much the worse to be kept secret, sir.

Alib.

Why, now thou meet'st the substance of the point:
I am old, Lollio.

Lol.

No, sir, 'tis I am old Lollio.   20

Alib.

Yet why may not this concord and sympathize?
Old trees and young plants often grow together,
Well enough agreeing.

---

3. *close to*] Close-mouthed about.
15. *'Tis . . . about*] That's what I'm about to do.

Lol.

Ay, sir, but the old trees raise themselves higher and
broader than the young plants.   25

Alib.

Shrewd application! There's the fear, man:
I would wear my ring on my own finger;
Whilst it is borrowed it is none of mine,
But his that useth it.

Lol.

You must keep it on still, then; if it but lie by, one or   30
other will be thrusting into't.

Alib.

Thou conceiv'st me, Lollio; here thy watchful eye
Must have employment. I cannot always be
At home.

Lol.

I dare swear you cannot.   35

Alib.

I must look out.

Lol.

I know't, you must look out; 'tis every man's case.

Alib.

Here, I do say, must thy employment be:
To watch her treadings, and in my absence
Supply my place.   40

Lol.

I'll do my best, sir; yet surely I cannot see who you
should have cause to be jealous of.

---

26. *Shrewd application*] Because the cuckold's horns make the
husband's head higher and broader than his wife's (Dilke).

27.] A charm against cuckolding.

32. *Thou . . . me*] "You get me."

39. *treadings*] Comings and goings.

42. *jealous*] Suspicious.

Alib.

Thy reason for that, Lollio? 'Tis a comfortable question.

Lol.

We have but two sorts of people in the house, and both
under the whip: that's fools and madmen. The one has   45
not wit enough to be knaves and the other not knavery
enough to be fools.

Alib.

Ay, those are all my patients, Lollio.
I do profess the cure of either sort:
My trade, my living 'tis; I thrive by it.   50
But here's the care that mixes with my thrift:
The daily visitants that come to see
My brainsick patients I would not have
To see my wife. Gallants I do observe
Of quick, enticing eyes, rich in habits,   55
Of stature and proportion very comely:
These are most shrewd temptations, Lollio.

Lol.

They may be easily answered, sir: if they come to see
the fools and madmen, you and I may serve the turn;
and let my mistress alone: she's of neither sort.   60

Alib.

'Tis a good ward. Indeed, come they to see
Our madmen or our fools, let 'em see no more
Than what they come for; by that consequent

---

49. *I do profess*] My profession is.

52. *daily visitants*] Tours of lunatic asylums were a common
form of entertainment.

55. *habits*] Clothes.

57. *shrewd*] "Sore."

59. *you . . . turn*] You're a fool, and I can pretend to be
mad.

60. *let . . . alone*] Don't worry about my mistress.

61. *ward*] Defense (in duelling).

They must not see her. I'm sure she's no fool.

Lol.

And I'm sure she's no madman.   65

Alib.

Hold that buckler fast, Lollio; my trust
Is on thee, and I account it firm and strong.
What hour is't, Lollio?

Lol.

Towards belly hour, sir.

Alib.

Dinner time? Thou mean'st twelve o'clock?   70

Lol.

Yes, sir, for every part has his hour: we wake at six and
look about us, that's eye hour; at seven we should pray,
that's knee hour; at eight walk, that's leg hour; at nine
gather flowers and pluck a rose, that's nose hour; at ten
we drink, that's mouth hour; at eleven lay about us for   75
victuals, that's hand hour; at twelve go to dinner, that's
belly hour.

Alib.

Profoundly, Lollio! It will be long
Ere all thy scholars learn this lesson; and
I did look to have a new one ent'red—stay,   80
I think my expectation is come home.
        Enter PEDRO, *and* ANTONIO *like an idiot.*

Ped.

Save you, sir. My business speaks itself;
This sight takes off the labor of my tongue.

---

66. *buckler*] Shield; cf. "ward," in l. 61.

69.] Nearly dinner time by my stomach.

71. *his*] Its.

74. *pluck a rose*] Relieve ourselves.

81.1. *like an idiot*] Probably wearing a long-skirted coat and
high, conical cap, and dangling from his wrist a child's primer
(Sampson).

Alib.

Ay, ay, sir,
'Tis plain enough you mean him for my patient.   85

Ped.

And if your pains prove but commodious to give but
some little strength to his sick and weak part of nature
in him, these are [*gives money*] but patterns to show
you of the whole pieces that will follow to you, beside
the charge of diet, washing, and other necessaries fully
defrayed.   90

Alib.

Believe it, sir, there shall no care be wanting.

Lol.

Sir, an officer in this place may deserve something; the
trouble will pass through my hands.

Ped.

'Tis fit something should come to your hands, then, sir.
                                        [*Gives him money.*]

Lol.

Yes, sir, 'tis I must keep him sweet, and read to him.
What is his name?   96

Ped.

His name is Antonio; marry, we use but half to him,
only Tony.

Lol.

Tony, Tony; 'tis enough, and a very good name for a
fool. What's your name, Tony?   100

Ant.

He, he, he! Well, I thank you, cousin. He, he, he!

---

86. *commodious to give*] Helpful in giving.

88. *patterns*] Samples, small change as compared to the whole
pieces in l. 89.

95. *sweet*] Clean, sweet-smelling.

97. *marry*] By Mary.

99–100. *Tony*] Later a synonym for fool. *OED* regards this
play as the possible origin.

Lol.

Good boy! Hold up your head. He can laugh; I perceive
by that he is no beast.

Ped.

Well, sir,
If you can raise him but to any height,   105
Any degree of wit; might he attain,
As I might say, to creep but on all four
Towards the chair of wit, or walk on crutches,
'Twould add an honor to your worthy pains
And a great family might pray for you,   110
To which he should be heir, had he discretion
To claim and guide his own. Assure you, sir,
He is a gentleman.

Lol.

Nay, there's nobody doubted that; at first sight I knew
him for a gentleman; he looks no other yet.   115

Ped.

Let him have good attendance and sweet lodging.

Lol.

As good as my mistress lies in, sir; and as you allow us
time and means, we can raise him to the higher degree
of discretion.

Ped.

Nay, there shall no cost want, sir.   120

Lol.

He will hardly be stretch'd up to the wit of a magnifico.

Ped.

O, no, that's not to be expected; far shorter will be
enough.

Lol.

I'll warrant you I make him fit to bear office in five

102–3. *he . . . beast*] A belief at least as old as Aristotle.
112. *guide his own*] Manage his inheritance.
116. *sweet*] Clean, sweet-smelling.
121. *hardly*] Hard-ly, with difficulty.

weeks; I'll undertake to wind him up to the wit of   125
constable.

Ped.

If it be lower than that it might serve turn.

Lol.

No, fie, to level him with a headborough, beadle, or
watchman were but little better than he is; constable
I'll able him. If he do come to be a justice afterwards,   130
let him thank the keeper. Or I'll go further with you:
say I do bring him up to my own pitch, say I make
him as wise as myself.

Ped.

Why, there I would have it.

Lol.

Well, go to, either I'll be as arrant a fool as he, or he   135
shall be as wise as I, and then I think 'twill serve his turn.

Ped.

Nay, I do like thy wit passing well.

Lol.

Yes, you may; yet if I had not been a fool, I had had
more wit than I have, too. Remember what state you
find me in.

Ped.

I will, and so leave you. Your best cares, I beseech you.   140

126–30. *constable . . . headborough . . . beadle . . . watchman*]
The incompetence of town and parish officials was an unfailing
object of satire.

127. *serve turn*] Be sufficient, "do." Cf. l. 136, below, and II.
ii.69.

129–30. *constable . . . him*] I'll fit him to be a constable.

134. *there . . . it*] I would have his wit as high as that.

135. *go to*] "All right, confound it!"
         arrant] Absolute.

137. *passing*] (Sur)passing(ly).

139. *state*] Status.

Alib.

Take you none with you, leave 'em all with us.

Exit PEDRO.

Ant.

O, my cousin's gone! Cousin, cousin, O!

Lol.

Peace, peace, Tony; you must not cry, child, you must
be whipp'd if you do. Your cousin is here still: I am
your cousin, Tony.   145

Ant.

He, he, then I'll not cry if thou be'st my cousin, he, he,
he.

Lol.

I were best try his wit a little, that I may know what
form to place him in.

Alib.

Ay, do, Lollio, do.   150

Lol.

I must ask him easy questions at first.—Tony, how
many true fingers has a tailor on his right hand?

Ant.

As many as on his left, cousin.

Lol.

Good; and how many on both?

Ant.

Two less than a deuce, cousin.   155

Lol.

Very well answered. I come to you again, cousin Tony:
how many fools goes to a wise man?

___

141. *none*] No cares.

148. *form*] Grade in the school.

152. *true*] Honest. Tailors were proverbially untrustworthy.

157. *fools goes to*] 1) Go to make; 2) visit. The singular verb
after a plural noun is common in Elizabethan grammar; cf. l.
200, below, II.ii.9–10, III.iii.84.

Ant.

Forty in a day sometimes, cousin.

Lol.

Forty in a day? How prove you that?

Ant.

All that fall out amongst themselves and go to a lawyer   160
to be made friends.

Lol.

A parlous fool! He must sit in the fourth form at least,
I perceive that.—I come again, Tony: how many
knaves make an honest man?

Ant.

I know not that, cousin.   165

Lol.

No, the question is too hard for you. I'll tell you,
cousin: there's three knaves may make an honest man,
a sergeant, a jailer, and a beadle; the sergeant catches
him, the jailer holds him, and the beadle lashes him;
and if he be not honest then, the hangman must cure
him.   170

Ant.

Ha, ha, ha, that's fine sport, cousin.

Alib.

This was too deep a question for the fool, Lollio.

Lol.

Yes, this might have serv'd yourself, though I say't.—
Once more, and you shall go play, Tony.

Ant.

Ay, play at push-pin, cousin, ha, he!   175

Lol.

So thou shalt. Say how many fools are here.

Ant.

Two, cousin, thou and I.

---

162. *parlous*] Perilous, dangerously clever.
175. *push-pin*] A child's game.

Lol.

Nay, y'are too forward there, Tony; mark my question:
how many fools and knaves are here? A fool before a
knave, a fool behind a knave, between every two fools   180
a knave: how many fools, how many knaves?

Ant.

I never learnt so far, cousin.

Alib.

Thou putt'st too hard questions to him, Lollio.

Lol.

I'll make him understand it easily.—Cousin, stand there.

Ant.

Ay, cousin.   185

Lol.

Master, stand you next the fool.

Alib.

Well, Lollio.

Lol.

Here's my place. Mark, now, Tony: there a fool before
a knave.

Ant.

That's I, cousin.   190

Lol.

Here's a fool behind a knave; that's I. And between
us two fools there is a knave; that's my master. 'Tis
but we three, that's all.

Ant. We three, we three, cousin!   *Madmen within.*
1 Within.

Put's head i' th' pillory, the bread's too little.   195

---

178. *y'are too forward*] You go too fast.

187. *Well*] "All right."

192–3. *we three*] A practical joke in which two persons, pretending to be knaves or fools, trick another (here Alibius) into
making a third. Cf. *Twelfth Night* II.iii.16–17.

195. *Put's*] Put his, either Alibius' or Lollio's.

2 Within.

Fly, fly, and he catches the swallow.

3 Within.

Give her more onion, or the devil put the rope about
her crag.

Lol.

You may hear what time of day it is: the chimes of
Bedlam goes.   200

Alib.

Peace, peace, or the wire comes!

3 Within.

Cat whore, cat whore! Her Permasant, her Permasant.

Alib.

Peace, I say.—Their hour's come; they must be fed,
Lollio.   205

Lol.

There's no hope of recovery of that Welsh madman:
was undone by a mouse that spoil'd him a Permasant;
lost his wits for't.

Alib.

Go to your charge, Lollio, I'll to mine.

Lol.

Go you to your madmen's ward, let me alone with your   210
fools.

195–8. The first madman is complaining about the scanty
food; the second sounds hallucinated; the third, a Welshman,
cries for more onions or for a rope to hang him.

198. *crag*] Neck.

199. *chimes of Bedlam*] Hunger cries of the inmates of Bethle-
hem Hospital, the famous London asylum.

201. *wire*] Whip.

202. *Cat whore*] Debauched, worthless she-cat.

    Her] Stage Welsh for "my" (Sampson).

    Permasant] Parmesan cheese, a staple of the Welsh diet
(cf. "Welsh rabbit"), and of English humor at the expense of the
Welsh.

Alib.

And remember my last charge, Lollio.   *Exit.*

Lol.

Of which your patients do you think I am?—Come,
Tony, you must amongst your schoolfellows now.
There's pretty scholars amongst 'em, I can tell you;   215
there's some of 'em at *stultus, stulta, stultum.*

Ant.

I would see the madmen, cousin, if they would not bite
me.

Lol.

No, they shall not bite thee, Tony.

Ant.

They bite when they are at dinner, do they not, coz?   220

Lol.

They bite at dinner indeed, Tony. Well, I hope to get
credit by thee; I like thee the best of all the scholars
that ever I brought up, and thou shalt prove a wise
man or I'll prove a fool myself.   *Exeunt.*

---

212. *my last charge*] To spy on my wife (ll. 32–40, above).

213. *Of . . . am*] Do you think I am a madman or a fool?

215–16. *there's . . .* stultum] Some of them are learning the
declension of the Latin adjective "foolish."

ACTUS SECUNDUS

Enter BEATRICE *and* JASPERINO *severally.*

Bea.

O, sir, I'm ready now for that fair service
Which makes the name of friend sit glorious on you.
Good angels and this conduct be your guide!

[*Gives a paper.*]

Fitness of time and place is there set down, sir.

Jas.

The joy I shall return rewards my service.   *Exit.*   5

Bea.

How wise is Alsemero in his friend!
It is a sign he makes his choice with judgment.
Then I appear in nothing more approv'd
Than making choice of him;
For 'tis a principle: he that can choose   10
That bosom well who of his thoughts partakes
Proves most discreet in every choice he makes.

II.i.] An Apartment in Vermandero's Castle.
0.1 *severally*] Separately; often, at different doors.
3. *conduct*] Paper containing directions.
5. *return*] Take back to Alsemero.
8. *approv'd*] Justified.

Methinks I love now with the eyes of judgment
And see the way to merit, clearly see it.
A true deserver like a diamond sparkles: 15
In darkness you may see him; that's in absence,
Which is the greatest darkness falls on love;
Yet is he best discern'd then
With intellectual eyesight. What's Piracquo
My father spends his breath for? And his blessing   20
Is only mine as I regard his name;
Else it goes from me and turns head against me,
Transform'd into a curse. Some speedy way
Must be rememb'red. He's so forward, too,
So urgent that way, scarce allows me breath   25
To speak to my new comforts.
                    Enter DE FLORES.

De F. [*aside.*]   Yonder's she.
Whatever ails me, now a-late especially,
I can as well be hang'd as refrain seeing her;
Some twenty times a day—nay, not so little—
Do I force errands, frame ways and excuses   30
To come into her sight; and I have small reason for't
And less encouragement, for she baits me still
Every time worse than other; does profess herself
The cruelest enemy to my face in town;

---

17. *falls*] That falls.

19–20. *Piracquo My*] Piracquo whom My.

20–1. *his blessing . . . name*] My father's blessing is mine
only as I enhance the family name by marrying Alonzo.

23–4. *Some . . . rememb'red*] I must bear in mind the devising
of some quick way out of my predicament.

24. *He's*] Alonzo is. Cf. I.i.188–9.

    forward] Importunate.

26. *new comforts*] Alsemero. The entrance of De Flores is
thus doubly ironical.

27. *a-late*] Of late.

At no hand can abide the sight of me,   35
As if danger or ill luck hung in my looks.
I must confess my face is bad enough,
But I know far worse has better fortune,
And not endur'd alone, but doted on;
And yet such pick-hair'd faces, chins like witches',   40
Here and there five hairs whispering in a corner
As if they grew in fear one of another,
Wrinkles like troughs, where swine-deformity swills
The tears of perjury that lie there like wash
Fallen from the slimy and dishonest eye—   45
Yet such a one pluck'd sweets without restraint
And has the grace of beauty to his sweet.
Though my hard fate has thrust me out to servitude,
I tumbled into th' world a gentleman.—
She turns her blessed eye upon me now   50
And I'll endure all storms before I part with't.
Bea.   [*aside.*]
Again!
This ominous, ill-fac'd fellow more disturbs me
Than all my other passions.
De F.   [*aside.*]
                              Now't begins again;
I'll stand this storm of hail though the stones pelt me. 55
Bea.
Thy business? What's thy business?
De F.   [*aside.*]
                              Soft and fair!
I cannot part so soon now.

---

35. *At no hand*] By no means, or perhaps, Neither close to
nor at a distance.
   38. *worse has*] Worse faces that have.
   39. *not . . . alone*] Not just endured.
   40. *pick-hair'd*] Patchily bearded.
   47. *to his sweet*] In his sweetheart's eyes (Spencer).
   54. *passions*] Troubles (Schelling).
   56. *Soft and fair*] Walk softly, speak her fair.

Bea.   [*aside.*]
                                The villain's fix'd.—
Thou standing toadpool!
De F.   [*aside.*]
                         The shower falls amain now.
Bea.
Who sent thee? What's thy errand? Leave my sight.
De F.
My lord your father charg'd me to deliver   60
A message to you.
Bea.   What, another since?
Do't and be hang'd, then; let me be rid of thee.
De F.
True service merits mercy.
Bea.   What's thy message?
De F.
Let beauty settle but in patience,
You shall hear all.
Bea.   A dallying, trifling torment!   65
De F.
Signor Alonzo de Piracquo, lady,
Sole brother to Tomazo de Piracquo—
Bea.
Slave, when wilt make an end?
De F.   [*aside.*]
                            Too soon I shall.
Bea.
What all this while of him?
De F.   The said Alonzo,
With the foresaid Tomazo—
Bea.   Yet again?   70
De F.
Is new alighted.

---

57. *fix'd*] Immovable.
58. *standing*] 1) Fixed; 2) stagnant.
    amain] Full force.
61. *since*] Cf. I.i.93ff.

Bea.   Vengeance strike the news!
    Thou thing most loath'd, what cause was there in this
    To bring thee to my sight?
De F.   My lord your father
    Charg'd me to seek you out.
Bea.   Is there no other
    To send his errand by?
De F.   It seems 'tis my luck   75
    To be i' th' way still.
Bea.   Get thee from me.
De F.   So!
    [*Aside.*] Why, am not I an ass to devise ways
    Thus to be rail'd at? I must see her still!
    I shall have a mad qualm within this hour again,
    I know't; and like a common Garden bull   80
    I do but take breath to be lugg'd again.
    What this may bode I know not; I'll despair the less
    Because there's daily precedents of bad faces
    Belov'd beyond all reason; these foul chops
    May come into favor one day 'mongst his fellows.   85
    Wrangling has prov'd the mistress of good pastime;
    As children cry themselves asleep, I ha' seen
    Women have chid themselves abed to men.
                    Exit DE FLORES.
Bea.
    I never see this fellow but I think
    Of some harm towards me; danger's in my mind still; 90
    I scarce leave trembling of an hour after.
    The next good mood I find my father in

---

79. *mad qualm*] Pang of lust.

80–1. *Garden*] Paris Garden, where bulls were tethered and "lugg'd" (l. 81), i.e. torn by savage dogs.

84. *these foul chops*] My ugly mouth and cheeks.

88. *have*] Who have.

91. *of*] For.

I'll get him quite discarded. O, I was
Lost in this small disturbance and forgot
Affliction's fiercer torment that now comes   95
To bear down all my comforts.

Enter VERMANDERO, ALONZO, TOMAZO.

Ver.   Y'are both welcome,
But an especial one belongs to you, sir,
To whose most noble name our love presents
The addition of a son: our son Alonzo.

Alon.
The treasury of honor cannot bring forth   100
A title I should more rejoice in, sir.

Ver.
You have improv'd it well.—Daughter, prepare:
The day will steal upon thee suddenly.

Bea.   [*aside.*]
Howe'er, I will be sure to keep the night
If it should come so near me.

[BEATRICE *and* VERMANDERO *talk apart.*]

Tom.   Alonzo.

Alon.   Brother?   105

Tom.
In troth, I see small welcome in her eye.

Alon.
Fie, you are too severe a censurer
Of love in all points; there's no bringing on you

---

96. *comforts*] Alsemero. Cf. l. 26, above.

97. *one*] Welcome.

98. *our*] The "royal plural" indicates Vermandero's high sense
of rank.

99. *addition*] Title.

104. *keep the night*] Mount all-night guard, deny myself to
Alonzo.

107. *censurer*] Judge.

108. *bringing on you*] Making you see that.

If lovers should mark everything a fault,
Affection would be like an ill-set book   110
Whose faults might prove as big as half the volume.
                [TOMAZO *and* ALONZO *talk apart.*]
Bea.
That's all I do entreat.
Ver.   It is but reasonable;
I'll see what my son says to't.—Son Alonzo,
Here's a motion made but to reprieve
A maidenhead three days longer; the request   115
Is not far out of reason, for indeed
The former time is pinching.
Alon.   Though my joys
Be set back so much time as I could wish
They had been forward, yet since she desires it
The time is set as pleasing as before;   120
I find no gladness wanting.
Ver.
May I ever meet it in that point still!
Y'are nobly welcome, sirs.
                Exeunt VERMANDERO *and* BEATRICE.
Tom.
So!—
Did you mark the dulness of her parting now?   125
Alon.
What dulness? Thou art so exceptious still!
Tom.
Why, let it go, then; I am but a fool
To mark your harms so heedfully.

---

110. *ill-set*] Full of typesetter's errors.

111. *faults*] Errata, list of corrections (Schelling).

117. *The . . . pinching*] The earlier date (I.i.189) is uncomfortably pressing.

126. *exceptious*] Full of objections (in the courtroom sense).

128. *your harms*] These discourtesies to you.

Alon.   Where's the oversight?
Tom.

    Come, your faith's cozened in her, strongly cozened;
    Unsettle your affection with all speed   130
    Wisdom can bring it to; your peace is ruin'd else.
    Think what a torment 'tis to marry one
    Whose heart is leapt into another's bosom.
    If ever pleasure she receive from thee,
    It comes not in thy name or of thy gift;   135
    She lies but with another in thine arms,
    He the half-father unto all thy children
    In the conception; if he get 'em not,
    She helps to get 'em for him, in his passions.
    And how dangerous   140
    And shameful her restraint may go in time to,
    It is not to be thought on without sufferings.
Alon.

    You speak as if she lov'd some other, then.
Tom.

    Do you apprehend so slowly?
Alon.   Nay, an that
    Be your fear only, I am safe enough.   145
    Preserve your friendship and your counsel, brother,
    For times of more distress; I should depart
    An enemy, a dangerous, deadly one
    To any but thyself that should but think
    She knew the meaning of inconstancy,   150

---

    134. *pleasure*] Sexual enjoyment.

    138–9. *get*] Beget.

    139.] This line is so difficult to explain that most editors omit
"in his passions." I take *him* as the lover, *his* as the husband's.

    140. *And how dangerous*] See the Introduction, p. 9.

    140-1. *And how . . . to*] How dangerous and shameful such
suppression of her feelings may ultimately become.

    144. *an*] If.

Much less the use and practice. Yet w'are friends.
Pray let no more be urg'd; I can endure
Much, till I meet an injury to her;
Then I am not myself. Farewell, sweet brother;
How much w'are bound to heaven to depart lovingly!
                                                   Exit.

Tom.

  Why, here is love's tame madness; thus a man   156
  Quickly steals into his vexation.   *Exit.*

[II.ii]

            Enter DIAPHANTA *and* ALSEMERO.

Dia.

The place is my charge; you have kept your hour,
And the reward of a just meeting bless you.
I hear my lady coming. Complete gentleman,
I dare not be too busy with my praises,
Th'are dangerous things to deal with.   *Exit.*

Als.   This goes well;   5

These women are the ladies' cabinets,
Things of most precious trust are lock'd into 'em.

              Enter BEATRICE.

Bea.

I have within mine eye all my desires;

---

151. *Yet w'are friends*] We are still friends.

155. *bound*] Indebted.

     to depart] That we part. See l. 151, above.

157. *vexation*] Trouble.

II.ii.] Another Apartment in Vermandero's Castle.

1. *my charge*] My responsibility.

2. *just*] Right and proper. Diaphanta sympathizes in the intrigue.

3. *Complete*] Perfect.

5. *dangerous*] If Beatrice should learn of them.

6. *cabinets*] Confidantes.

Requests that holy prayers ascend heaven for,
And brings 'em down to furnish our defects 10
Come not more sweet to our necessities
Than thou unto my wishes.

Als. W'are so like

In our expressions, lady, that unless I borrow
The same words I shall never find their equals.

[*Kisses her.*]

Bea.

How happy were this meeting, this embrace, 15
If it were free from envy! This poor kiss,
It has an enemy, a hateful one,
That wishes poison to't. How well were I now
If there were none such name known as Piracquo
Nor no such tie as the command of parents! 20
I should be but too much blessèd.

Als. One good service

Would strike off both your fears, and I'll go near it, too,
Since you are so distress'd: remove the cause,
The command ceases; so there's two fears blown out
With one and the same blast.

Bea. Pray, let me find you, sir. 25
What might that service be, so strangely happy?

Als.

The honorablest piece 'bout man, valor.
I'll send a challenge to Piracquo instantly.

---

10. *furnish our defects*] Supply what we lack.
16. *envy*] Hate.
21. *service*] See l. 28, below.
22. *go near it*] Make a good guess at what it is.
23. *cause*] Piracquo (l. 19).
24. *command*] Cf. l. 20, above.
25. *find you*] Discover your meaning.
26. *happy*] Fortunate in its results.
27. *piece 'bout*] Part of.

Bea.

How? Call you that extinguishing of fear
When 'tis the only way to keep it flaming?   30
Are not you ventured in the action,
That's all my joys and comforts? Pray, no more, sir.
Say you prevail'd, y'are danger's and not mine, then;
The law would claim you from me, or obscurity
Be made the grave to bury you alive.   35
I'm glad these thoughts come forth; O, keep not one
Of this condition, sir; here was a course
Found to bring sorrow on her way to death;
The tears would ne'er ha' dried till dust had chok'd 'em.
Blood-guiltiness becomes a fouler visage—   40
[*Aside.*] And now I think on one! I was to blame
I ha' marr'd so good a market with my scorn.
'T had been done questionless; the ugliest creature
Creation fram'd for some use; yet to see
I could not mark so much where it should be!   45

Als.

Lady—

Bea.   [*aside.*]
          Why, men of art make much of poison:
Keep one to expel another. Where was my art?

Als.

Lady, you hear not me.

Bea.   I do especially, sir;
The present times are not so sure of our side

---

32. *That's*] You who are.

34. *obscurity*] Hiding or exile.

41. *one*] One fouler visage, De Flores'.

42. *I ha' . . . market*] For having passed up so good a deal.

43. *'T . . . questionless*] He'd have done it without question.

45.] I could not so much as notice what use might be found
for De Flores.

46, 47. *art*] Science, cunning.

49. *sure of*] Surely on.

As those hereafter may be; we must use 'em, then,   50
As thrifty folks their wealth: sparingly now
Till the time opens.

Als.   You teach wisdom, lady.

Bea.

Within, there! Diaphanta!

           Reenter DIAPHANTA.

Dia.   Do you call, madam?

Bea.

Perfect your service and conduct this gentleman
The private way you brought him.

Dia.   I shall, madam.   55

Als.

My love's as firm as love e'er built upon.

           Exeunt DIAPHANTA *and* ALSEMERO.
           Enter DE FLORES.

De F.   [*aside.*]

I have watch'd this meeting and do wonder much
What shall become of t'other; I'm sure both
Cannot be serv'd unless she transgress; happily,
Then, I'll put in for one; for if a woman   60
Fly from one point, from him she makes a husband,
She spreads and mounts then like arithmetic,
One, ten, a hundred, a thousand, ten thousand,
Proves in time sutler to an army royal.
Now do I look to be most richly rail'd at,   65
Yet I must see her.

Bea.   [*aside.*]
           Why, put case I loath'd him

---

52. *the time opens*] Our time comes.

54. *and conduct*] By conducting.

58. *t'other*] Alonzo.

59–60. *happily . . . one*] Perchance, then, I'll apply for a share.

64. *sutler*] One who follows an army to sell things to the troops.

66. *put case*] Suppose.

As much as youth and beauty hates a sepulcher,
Must I needs show it? Cannot I keep that secret
And serve my turn upon him? See, he's here.—
De Flores.

De F.   [*aside.*]
                              Ha, I shall run mad with joy: 70
She call'd me fairly by my name, De Flores,
And neither rogue nor rascal!

Bea.   What ha' you done
To your face a-late? Y'have met with some good physician;
Y'have prun'd yourself, methinks; you were not wont
To look so amorously.

De F.   [*aside.*]
                                            Not I;   75
'Tis the same physnomy, to a hair and pimple,
Which she call'd scurvy scarce an hour ago.
How is this?

Bea.   Come hither. Nearer, man!

De F.   [*aside.*]
I'm up to the chin in heaven.

Bea.   Turn, let me see.
Faugh, 'tis but the heat of the liver, I perceive't.   80
I thought it had been worse.

De F.   [*aside.*]
                              Her fingers touch'd me!
She smells all amber.

Bea.
I'll make a water for you shall cleanse this
Within a fortnight.

---

69. *serve . . . him*] Use him for my own ends.
74. *prun'd*] Preened, made more attractive.
75. *amorously*] Lovable.
     Not I] I've done nothing to improve my looks.
76. *physnomy*] Phys(iog)nomy.
82. *amber*] Alluring.

De F.   With your own hands, lady?

Bea.

Yes, mine own, sir; in a work of cure   85
I'll trust no other.

De F.   [*aside.*]
'Tis half an act of pleasure
To hear her talk thus to me.

Bea.   When w'are us'd
To a hard face, 'tis not so unpleasing;
It mends still in opinion, hourly mends;
I see it by experience.

De F.   [*aside.*]
I was blest   90
To light upon this minute; I'll make use on't.

Bea.

Hardness becomes the visage of a man well:
It argues service, resolution, manhood,
If cause were of employment.

De F.   'Twould be soon seen
If e'er your ladyship had cause to use it.   95
I would but wish the honor of a service
So happy as that mounts to.

Bea.   We shall try you—
O, my De Flores!

De F.   [*aside.*]
How's that?
She calls me hers already: "my" De Flores!—
You were about to sigh out somewhat, madam.   100

Bea.

No, was I? I forgot—O!

De F.   There 'tis again,
The very fellow on't.

---

86. *pleasure*] Sex.
88, 92. *hard . . . Hardness*] Ugly . . . Ugliness.
102. *on't*] Of her previous sigh.

Bea.   You are too quick, sir.
De F.

There's no excuse for't now, I heard it twice, madam;
That sigh would fain have utterance; take pity on't
And lend it a free word; 'las, how it labors   105
For liberty! I hear the murmur yet
Beat at your bosom.
Bea.   Would creation—
De F.

Ay, well said, that's it.
Bea.   Had form'd me man!
De F.

Nay, that's not it.
Bea.   O, 'tis the soul of freedom!
I should not then be forc'd to marry one   110
I hate beyond all depths; I should have power
Then to oppose my loathings, nay remove 'em
Forever from my sight.
De F.   O blest occasion!
Without change to your sex, you have your wishes.
Claim so much man in me.
Bea.   In thee, De Flores?   115
There's small cause for that.
De F.   Put it not from me;
It's a service that I kneel for to you.   [*Kneels.*]
Bea.

You are too violent to mean faithfully;
There's horror in my service, blood and danger;
Can those be things to sue for?
De F.   If you knew   120
How sweet it were to me to be employed
In any act of yours, you would say then

---

103. *excuse*] Evasion.

122–4. *you . . . on't*] When I receive instructions for the act,
you will say I didn't sue humbly enough.

I fail'd and us'd not reverence enough,
When I receive the charge on't.
Bea.   [*aside.*]
                              This is much, methinks;
Belike his wants are greedy, and to such   125
Gold tastes like angels' food.—Rise.
De F.
I'll have the work first.
Bea.   [*aside.*]
                                          Possible his need
Is strong upon him. [*Gives him money.*]—There's to
    encourage thee:
As thou art forward and thy service dangerous,
Thy reward shall be precious.
De F.   That I have thought on;   130
I have assur'd myself of that beforehand
And know it will be precious. The thought ravishes!
Bea.
Then take him to thy fury.
De F.   I thirst for him.
Bea.
Alonzo de Piracquo.
De F.   [*rising.*]
                              His end's upon him;
He shall be seen no more.
Bea.   How lovely now   135
Dost thou appear to me! Never was man
Dearlier rewarded.
De F.   I do think of that.
Bea.
Be wondrous careful in the execution.

---

129. *As . . . forward*] In proportion as you are aggressive.
137. *rewarded*] I.e. than you shall be.

De F.

Why? Are not both our lives upon the cast?

Bea.

Then I throw all my fears upon thy service.   140

De F.

They ne'er shall rise to hurt you.

Bea.   When the deed's done,

I'll furnish thee with all things for thy flight;

Thou may'st live bravely in another country.

De F.

Ay, ay, we'll talk of that hereafter.

Bea.   [*aside.*]

                    I shall rid myself

Of two inveterate loathings at one time: 145

Piracquo and His Dogface.   *Exit.*

De F.   O, my blood!

Methinks I feel her in mine arms already,

Her wanton fingers combing out this beard,

And, being pleasèd, praising this bad face.

Hunger and pleasure! They'll commend sometimes   150

Slovenly dishes, and feed heartily on 'em;

Nay, which is stranger, refuse daintier for 'em.

Some women are odd feeders.—I'm too loud:

Here comes the man goes supperless to bed

Yet shall not rise tomorrow to his dinner.   155

Enter ALONZO

Alon.

De Flores.

---

139. *Why?*] What need to tell me that?

    upon the cast] At stake.

143. *bravely*] Handsomely.

146. *His Dogface*] De Flores.

    O, my blood] Cf. II.i.79n.

150.] How powerful are hunger and sexual desire! Because of them women will sometimes relish . . .

154. *goes*] Who shall go.

De F.   My kind, honorable lord?

Alon.

I am glad I ha' met with thee.

De F.   Sir?

Alon.   Thou canst show me

The full strength of the castle?

De F.   That I can, sir.

Alon.

I much desire it.

De F.   And if the ways and straits

Of some of the passages be not too tedious for you,   160

I will assure you worth your time and sight, my lord.

Alon.

Puh, that shall be no hindrance.

De F.   I'm your servant, then.

'Tis now near dinner time; 'gainst your lordship's rising

I'll have the keys about me.

Alon.   Thanks, kind De Flores.

De. F.   [*aside.*]

He's safely thrust upon me, beyond hopes.   *Exeunt.*   165

---

159. *ways*] Long passages.

     straits] Narrow passages.

160. *tedious*] Tiresome.

161. *worth*] I.e. the tour will be worth.

162. *that*] Those difficulties.

163–4. *'gainst . . . rising*] By the time your lordship rises from table.

165.] Better than I could have hoped! He's put himself into my hands; I can safely murder him, for no one else knows where he is (III.ii.3–5).

ACTUS TERTIUS

[III.i]

Enter ALONZO *and* DE FLORES.
(*In the act-time* DE FLORES *hides a naked rapier.*)

De F.
    Yes, here are all the keys; I was afraid, my lord,
    I'd wanted for the postern. This is it.
    I've all, I've all, my lord; this for the sconce.
Alon.
    'Tis a most spacious and impregnable fort.
De F.
    You'll tell me more, my lord.—This descent   5
    Is somewhat narrow; we shall never pass
    Well with our weapons, they'll but trouble us.
Alon.
    Thou say'st true.

III.i.] A Narrow Passage in Vermandero's Castle.

0.2. *act-time*] Intermission.

2. *wanted*] Lacked the key.

3. *sconce*] Here, perhaps, a small, detached fort; but see III.ii.13, below.

5. *You'll . . . more*] Because you haven't seen it all yet.

8. *help*] To remove your sword belt.

58

De F.   Pray, let me help your lordship.

Alon.

  'Tis done. Thanks, kind De Flores.

De F.   Here are hooks, my lord,

To hang such things on purpose.

                         [He hangs up the swords.]

Alon.   Lead, I'll follow thee.   10

        Exeunt at one door and enter at the other.

[III.ii.]

De F.

  All this is nothing; you shall see anon

  A place you little dream on.

Alon.   I am glad

  I have this leisure. All your master's house

  Imagine I ha' taken a gondola.

De F.

  All but myself, sir, *[aside]* which makes up my safety.—   5

  My lord, I'll place you at a casement here

  Will show you the full strength of all the castle.

  Look, spend your eye awhile upon that object.

Alon.

  Here's rich variety, De Flores.

De F.   Yes, sir.

Alon.

  Goodly munition.

    10.1.] A common stage device to indicate a change in location, here to a descent (l. 5, above) leading to an underground passage and vault.

    III.ii.] A Vault.

    6. *casement*] This casement may be supposed to look outward toward the fortifications, with ordnance in place, so that the sconce, a small, separate fort for which De Flores has the key (III.i.3), is visible to Alonzo.

    7, 11. *will*] Which will.

De F.   Ay, there's ordnance, sir,   10
  No bastard metal; will ring you a peal like bells
  At great men's funerals.—Keep your eye straight, my lord;
  Take special notice of that sconce before you:
  There you may dwell awhile.   [*Takes up the rapier.*]
Alon.   I am upon't.
De F.
  And so am I.   [*Stabs him.*]
Alon.   De Flores! O, De Flores,   15
  Whose malice hast thou put on?
De F.   Do you question
  A work of secrecy? I must silence you.   [*Stabs him.*]
Alon.

  O, O, O!
De F.   I must silence you.   [*Stabs him.*]
  So! Here's an undertaking well accomplish'd.
  This vault serves to good use now.—Ha! What's that   20
  Threw sparkles in my eye? O, 'tis a diamond
  He wears upon his finger. It was well found:
  This will approve the work. What, so fast on?
  Not part in death? I'll take a speedy course, then;   24
  Finger and all shall off. [*Cuts off the finger.*] So! Now
    I'll clear
  The passages from all suspect or fear.   *Exit with body.*

---

11. *bastard*] Base.
13. *sconce*] See the note on l. 6.
    I . . . it] I'm looking at it (the sconce).
15. *And . . . I*] And I'm ready to do it (the murder).
20. *vault*] See l. 6n.
23. *approve the work*] Prove I have done the job.
25–6. *clear . . . fear*] I.e. remove Alonzo's sword, belt, etc.

[III.iii]

Enter ISABELLA *and* LOLLIO.

Isa.

Why, sirrah? Whence have you commission
To fetter the doors against me?
If you keep me in a cage, pray whistle to me;
Let me be doing something.

Lol.

You shall be doing, if it please you; I'll whistle to you   5
if you'll pipe after.

Isa.

Is it your master's pleasure or your own
To keep me in this pinfold?

Lol.

'Tis for my master's pleasure, lest being taken in another man's corn you might be pounded in another place.   10

Isa.

'Tis very well, and he'll prove very wise.

Lol.

He says you have company enough in the house, if you
please to be sociable, of all sorts of people.

Isa.

Of all sorts? Why, here's none but fools and madmen.

Lol.

Very well. And where will you find any other if you   15
should go abroad? There's my master and I to boot, too.

III.iii.] An Apartment in Alibius' House.

6. *pipe after*] Whistle in return; i.e. cooperate in "doing."

8. *pinfold*] Pound for stray cattle "taken in another man's
corn" (ll. 9–10).

10. *pounded*] Impounded, with bawdy double meaning.

16. *abroad*] Out of the house.

Isa.

Of either sort one: a madman and a fool.

Lol.

I would ev'n participate of both, then, if I were as you;
I know y'are half mad already; be half foolish, too.

Isa.

Y'are a brave, saucy rascal! Come on, sir,   20
Afford me then the pleasure of your bedlam;
You were commending once today to me
Your last-come lunatic, what a proper
Body there was without brains to guide it,
And what a pitiful delight appear'd   25
In that defect, as if your wisdom had found
A mirth in madness. Pray, sir, let me partake,
If there be such a pleasure.

Lol.

If I do not show you the handsomest, discreetest madman, one that I may call the understanding madman,   30
then say I am a fool.

Isa.

Well, a match; I will say so.

Lol.

When you have a taste of the madman, you shall, if you
please, see Fool's College o' th' side. I seldom lock there;
'tis but shooting a bolt or two and you are amongst 'em.   35
                                           Exit. Reenter presently.
Come on, sir, let me see how handsomely you'll be-
have yourself now.

---

20. *brave*] Fine.
21. *bedlam*] Madhouse.
23. *proper*] Handsome.
32. *a match*] "It's a deal."
34. *o' th' side*] Also.

Enter FRANCISCUS.

Fran.

How sweetly she looks! O, but there's a wrinkle in her
brow as deep as philosophy. Anacreon, drink to my
mistress' health, I'll pledge it. Stay, stay, there's a
spider in the cup! No, 'tis but a grapestone. Swallow it,
fear nothing, poet; so, so, lift higher.

Isa.

Alack, alack, 'tis too full of pity
To be laugh'd at. How fell he mad? Canst thou tell?

Lol.

For love, mistress. He was a pretty poet, too, and that   45
set him forwards first; the Muses then forsook him; he
ran mad for a chambermaid, yet she was but a dwarf,
neither.

Fran.

Hail, bright Titania!
Why stand'st thou idle on these flow'ry banks?
Oberon is dancing with his Dryades;   50
I'll gather daisies, primrose, violets,
And bind them in a verse of poesie.

Lol.

Not too near! You see your danger.   [*Shows the whip.*]

Fran.

O, hold thy hand, great Diomed;

39–41. *Anacreon . . . it*] Anacreon is reported to have choked
on a grapestone while drinking a cup of wine. Franciscus, feign-
ing madness, pretends to be witnessing the incident.

41. *spider*] Believed poisonous.

47. *yet . . . neither*] Although she was only a dwarf at that.

48, 50. *Titania . . . Oberon*] Queen and king of the fairies in
A Midsummer Night's Dream and elsewhere. Franciscus is invit-
ing Isabella to an intrigue while Alibius-Oberon dallies with
other women (Dryades).

Thou feed'st thy horses well, they shall obey thee;   55
Get up, Bucephalus kneels.   [*Kneels.*]
Lol.
You see how I awe my flock; a shepherd has not his
dog at more obedience.
Isa.
His conscience is unquiet; sure that was
The cause of this. A proper gentleman.   60
Fran.
Come hither, Esculapius; hide the poison.   [*Rises.*]
Lol.
Well, 'tis hid.   [*Hides the whip.*]
Fran.
Didst thou never hear of one Tiresias,
A famous poet?
Lol.
Yes, that kept tame wild geese.   65
Fran.
That's he; I am the man.
Lol.
No!
Fran.
Yes; but make no words on't; I was a man
Seven years ago—
Lol.
A stripling, I think you might—   70

---

56. *Get up*] Mount.

60. *proper*] Handsome.

63. *Tiresias*] A legendary Theban soothsayer who was both
blind and second-sighted, man and woman. He was not known
as a poet (l. 64), but we do not expect accuracy from either
Franciscus or Lollio.

65. *tame wild geese*] Perhaps expressing disbelief; otherwise
the point of the joke seems to have been lost, except as it sur-
vives in "wild-goose chase," a futile enterprise.

Fran.

Now I'm a woman, all feminine.

Lol.

I would I might see that.

Fran.

Juno struck me blind.

Lol.

I'll ne'er believe that, for a woman, they say, has an
eye more than a man.   75

Fran.

I say she struck me blind.

Lol.

And Luna made you mad; you have two trades to beg
with.

Fran.

Luna is now big-bellied, and there's room
For both of us to ride with Hecate;   80
I'll drag thee up into her silver sphere
And there we'll kick the dog and beat the bush
That barks against the witches of the night;
The swift lycanthropi that walks the round,

---

70. *might* —] A word or words may have been dropped at
the end of this line, as elsewhere: *say* (Bawcutt) or *have been;*
but probably the garrulous pair interrupt each other.

77. *two trades*] Blindness and madness.

79. *big-bellied*] Full.

80. *Hecate*] A moon-goddess, later goddess of witchcraft. Her
name here has three syllables; in Shakespeare and earlier plays,
only two.

82. *dog . . . bush*] Where we "see" a man's face in the moon,
the Elizabethans saw a man with a bush, and a dog.

83. *barks*] Obviously the dog (l. 82), not the bush; but
"These are but wild and whirling words," like those of an earlier
pretended madman (*Hamlet* I.v.133).

We'll tear their wolvish skins and save the sheep.   85
                            [*Tries to seize* LOLLIO.]

Lol.

Is't come to this? Nay, then my poison comes forth
again; mad slave, indeed, abuse your keeper!

Isa.

I prithee hence with him now, he grows dangerous.

Fran.   *Sing.*

    Sweet love, pity me,
    Give me leave to lie with thee.   90

Lol.

No, I'll see you wiser first. To your own kennel!

Fran.

No noise, she sleeps; draw all the curtains round;
Let no soft sound molest the pretty soul
But love—and love creeps in at a mouse-hole.

Lol.

I would you would get into your hole.   95

                          Exit FRANCISCUS.

Now, mistress, I will bring you another sort. You shall
be fool'd another while.—Tony, come hither, Tony;
look who's yonder, Tony.

                Enter ANTONIO.

Ant.

Cousin, is it not my aunt?

Lol.

Yes, 'tis one of 'em, Tony.   100

Ant.

He, he! How do you, uncle?

Lol.

Fear him not, mistress, 'tis a gentle nigget; you may
play with him—as safely with him as with his bauble.

---

99. *aunt*] Slang for prostitute.
102. *nigget*] Fool.
103. *bauble*] An ass-head on a stick, carried by a court fool.

Isab.

How long hast thou been a fool?

Ant.

Ever since I came hither, cousin.   105

Isab.

Cousin! I'm none of thy cousins, fool.

Lol.

O, mistress, fools have always so much wit as to claim
their kindred.

Madman within.

Bounce, bounce! He falls, he falls!

Isa.

Hark you, your scholars in the upper room   110
Are out of order.

Lol.

Must I come amongst you there? Keep you the fool,
mistress; I'll go up and play left-handed Orlando
amongst the madmen.   *Exit.*

Isa.

Well, sir.   115

Ant.

'Tis opportuneful, now, sweet lady! Nay,
Cast no amazing eye upon this change.

Isa.

Ha!

---

105. *cousin*] Another insult like *aunt* (l. 99).

109. *Bounce, bounce!*] Bang, bang!

113. *left-handed*] clumsy, of inferior birth, or (Lawrence)
sinister. Sampson also notes that an illustration in Harington's
translation of Ariosto (1607) shows the hero holding his sword
in his left hand.

    Orlando] Hero of Ariosto's epic, *Orlando Furioso;* a mad,
terrifying fighter.

117. *amazing*] Beginning to show amazement.

    change] He drops the simpleton's voice and vacant look.

Ant.

    This shape of folly shrouds your dearest love,
    The truest servant to your powerful beauties,   120
    Whose magic had this force thus to transform me.

Isa.

    You are a fine fool indeed.

Ant.   O, 'tis not strange:

    Love has an intellect that runs through all
    The scrutinous sciences; and, like
    A cunning poet, catches a quantity   125
    Of every knowledge, yet brings all home
    Into one mystery, into one secret
    That he proceeds in.

Isa.   Y'are a parlous fool.

Ant.

    No danger in me: I bring naught but love
    And his soft-wounding shafts to strike you with.   130
    Try but one arrow; if it hurt you,
    I'll stand you twenty back in recompense.   [*Kisses her.*]

Isa.

    A forward fool, too.

Ant.   This was love's teaching:

    A thousand ways he fashioned out my way,
    And this I found the safest and [the] nearest   135
    To tread the Galaxia to my star.

Isa.

    Profound, withal! Certain, you dreamed of this;
    Love never taught it waking.

---

119. *shape*] Appearance, guise.
124. *scrutinous*] Investigative, searching.
127. *mystery*] Esoteric skill or knowledge.
133. *forward*] Presumptuous.
134. *he*] Cf. ll. 128, 130, above.
136. *Galaxia*] The Milky Way.
137. *withal*] Too (as well as *forward,* l. 133).

Ant.   Take no acquaintance
  Of these outward follies; there is within
  A gentleman that loves you.
Isa.   When I see him,   140
  I'll speak with him; so, in the meantime, keep
  Your habit; it becomes you well enough.
  As you are a gentleman, I'll not discover you;
  That's all the favor that you must expect.
  When you are weary you may leave the school,   145
  For all this while you have but play'd the fool.
                    Reenter LOLLIO.
Ant.
  And must again. He, he! I thank you, cousin:
  I'll be your valentine tomorrow morning.
Lol.
  How do you like the fool, mistress?
Isa.
  Passing well, sir.   150
Lol.
  Is he not witty—pretty well for a fool?
Isa.
  If he hold on as he begins, he is like
  To come to something.
Lol.
  Ay, thank a good tutor. You may put him to't; he
  begins to answer pretty hard questions. Tony, how   155
  many is five times six?
Ant.
  Five times six is six times five.

---

138. *Take no acquaintance*] Obviously, disregard; *OED* does
not list this meaning of *acquaintance.*
  142. *habit*] (Fool's) dress.
  143. *discover*] Betray.
  154. *put him to't*] Put him to questioning; examine him.

Lol.

What arithmetician could have answer'd better? How
many is one hundred and seven?

Ant.

One hundred and seven is seven hundred and one,   160
cousin.

Lol.

This is no wit to speak on. Will you be rid of the fool
now?

Isa.

By no means; let him stay a little.

Madman within.

Catch there, catch the last couple in hell!   165

Lol.

Again? Must I come amongst you? Would my master
were come home! I am not able to govern both these
wards together.   *Exit.*

Ant.

Why should a minute of love's hour be lost?

Isa.

Fie, out again! I had rather you kept   170
Your other posture: you become not your tongue
When you speak from your clothes.

Ant.   How can he freeze
Lives near so sweet a warmth? Shall I alone
Walk through the orchard of the Hesperides

165.] As in barley-break, a country game similar to prisoner's
base, played by three or more couples. The base was "hell." For
the connotation, see V.iii.163.

170. *out again*] Out of your role. Cf. *from your clothes,*
l. 172.

171. *posture*] Pose.

172. *from*] Not in accord with. See l. 170n.

173. *Lives*] Who lives.

And cowardly not dare to pull an apple?   175
This with the red cheeks I must venture for.
         [Tries to kiss her.]
     Enter LOLLIO *above.*

Isa.
Take heed, there's giants keep 'em.
Lol.   *[aside.]*
How now, fool, are you good at that? Have you
read Lipsius? He's past *Ars Amandi.* I believe I must
put harder questions to him; I perceive that—   180
Isa.
You are bold without fear, too.
Ant.   What should I fear,
Having all joys about me? Do you smile,
And love shall play the wanton on your lip,
Meet and retire, retire and meet again;
Look you but cheerfully, and in your eyes   185
I shall behold mine own deformity
And dress myself up fairer. I know this shape
Becomes me not, but in those bright mirrors
I shall array me handsomely.
Lol.
Cuckoo, cuckoo!   *Exit [above.]*   190
[Enter] Madmen above, some as birds, others as beasts.

---

177. *giants]* The part of Lollio may have been intended for a
large man; see also l. 199, below.

 'em] 1) The apples; 2) her cheeks.

179. *Lipsius]* Belgian classicist (1547–1606); used here for
the pun on "lips."

 He's . . . Amandi] Antonio has mastered Ovid's treatise
on the art of seduction.

182. *Do you smile]* A command: "Smile."

188. *mirrors]* Isabella's eyes.

190. *Cuckoo]* The call of the cuckoo in spring, suggesting
"cuckold."

Ant.

What are these?

Isa.   Of fear enough to part us;
Yet they are but our schools of lunatics,
That act their fantasies in any shapes
Suiting their present thoughts; if sad, they cry;
If mirth be their conceit, they laugh again;   195
Sometimes they imitate the beasts and birds,
Singing or howling, braying, barking—all
As their wild fancies prompt 'em.

                        [*Exeunt madmen above.*]
                   Reenter LOLLIO.

Ant.   These are no fears.
Isa.

But here's a large one: my man.
Ant.

Ha, he! That's fine sport indeed, cousin.   .   200
Lol.

I would my master were come home. 'Tis too much for
one shepherd to govern two of these flocks; nor can I
believe that one churchman can instruct two benefices
at once; there will be some incurable mad of the one
side and very fools on the other. Come, Tony.   205
Ant.

Prithee, cousin, let me stay here still.
Lol.

No, you must to your book now you have play'd
sufficiently.
Isa.

Your fool is grown wondrous witty.

---

194. *present*] Momentary.
195. *If . . . conceit*] If they're imagining something funny.
207. *now*] Now that.

Lol.

Well, I'll say nothing; but I do not think but he will put   210
you down one of these days.

       Exeunt LOLLIO *and* ANTONIO.

Isa.

Here the restrainèd current might make breach
Spite of the watchful bankers. Would a woman stray,
She need not gad abroad to seek her sin;
It would be brought home one ways or other.   215
The needle's point will to the fixèd north,
Such drawing arctics women's beauties are.

     Reenter LOLLIO.

Lol.

How dost thou, sweet rogue?

Isa.

How now?

Lol.

Come, there are degrees: one fool may be better than   220
another.

Isa.

What's the matter?

Lol.

Nay, if thou giv'st thy mind to fool's flesh, have at thee!

       [*Tries to kiss her.*]

210–11. *put you down*] 1) Outshine you in knowledge; 2) lie
with you.

213. *Spite of*] Despite.

  bankers] Workmen who repair the washed-out banks of
streams; here, of course, Alibius and Lollio.

  Would . . . stray] If a woman wishes to stray.

215. *brought home*] Accomplished. Cf. III.iv.71.

216. *will to*] Will turn toward.

217. *drawing arctics*] Magnetic poles.

Isa.

You bold slave, you!

Lol.

I could follow now as t'other fool did: 225
"What should I fear,
Having all joys about me? Do you but smile,
And love shall play the wanton on your lip,
Meet and retire, retire and meet again;
Look you but cheerfully, and in your eyes   230
I shall behold my own deformity
And dress myself up fairer; I know this shape
Becomes me not—" And so as it follows; but is not this
the more foolish way? Come, sweet rogue; kiss me, my
little Lacedemonian; let me feel how thy pulses beat.   235
Thou hast a thing about thee would do a man pleasure:
I'll lay my hand on't.

Isa.

Sirrah, no more! I see you have discovered
This love's knight errant, who hath made adventure
For purchase of my love. Be silent, mute,   240
Mute as a statue, or his injunction
For me enjoying shall be to cut thy throat.
I'll do it, though for no other purpose,
And be sure he'll not refuse it.

Lol.

My share, that's all; I'll have my fool's part with you.   245

Isa.

No more! Your master.

---

235. *Lacedemonian*] Spartan. Sampson suggests a similarity to
laced-mutton, slang for prostitute.

237. *lay*] 1) Place; 2) bet.

240. *For purchase of*] To gain.

Enter ALIBIUS

Alib.   Sweet, how dost thou?

Isa.

Your bounden servant, sir.

Alib.   Fie, fie, sweetheart,

No more of that.

Isa.   You were best lock me up.

Alib.

In my arms and bosom, my sweet Isabella,
I'll lock thee up most nearly. Lollio,   250
We have employment, we have task in hand:
At noble Vermandero's, our castle captain,
There is a nuptial to be solemniz'd—
Beatrice-Joanna, his fair daughter, bride—
For which the gentleman hath bespoke our pains;   255
A mixture of our madmen and our fools
To finish, as it were, and make the fag
Of all the revels, the third night from the first;
Only an unexpected passage over
To make a frightful pleasure, that is all,   260
But not the all I aim at; could we so act it
To teach it in a wild, distracted measure,
Though out of form and figure, breaking time's head,
It were no matter, 'twould be heal'd again
In one age or other, if not in this.   265

---

247. *Your . . . sir*] Spoken with mocking docility; cf. l. 2, above.

   bounden] 1) Faithful; 2) locked up.

257. *fag*] Fag end, the last and poorest part.

259. *over*] Over the stage, purportedly the ballroom floor.

260. *To . . . pleasure*] To give the revellers a pleasant scare.

262. *To teach it*] As to teach the madmen to do it.

263. *breaking time's head*] Making a cuckold of the musical rhythm. Cf. V.iii.213.

This, this, Lollio; there's a good reward begun,
And will beget a bounty, be it known.

Lol.

This is easy, sir, I'll warrant you. You have about you
fools and madmen that can dance very well; and 'tis no
wonder: your best dancers are not the wisest men; the   270
reason is, with often jumping they jolt their brains down
into their feet, that their wits lie more in their heels
than in their heads.

Alib.

Honest Lollio, thou giv'st me a good reason
And a comfort in it.

Isa.   Y'have a fine trade on't;   275
Madmen and fools are a staple commodity.

Alib.

O, wife, we must eat, wear clothes, and live;
Just at the lawyer's haven we arrive:
By madmen and by fools we both do thrive.   *Exeunt.*

[III.iv]

Enter VERMANDERO, ALSEMERO, JASPERINO, *and* BEATRICE.

Ver.

Valencia speaks so nobly of you, sir,
I wish I had a daughter now for you.

Als.

The fellow of this creature were a partner
For a king's love.

Ver.   I had her fellow once, sir,

---

266. *This*] (It will be healed in) this age; soon.
    there's . . . begun] We've made a start toward a large fee.
267. *be it known*] Let me tell you.
278. *lawyer's haven*] The security of the lawyer, who thrives
on people foolish or crazy enough to go to law.
III.iv.] An Apartment in the Castle.

But heaven has married her to joys eternal;　　　5
'Twere sin to wish her in this vale again.
Come, sir, your friend and you shall see the pleasures
Which my health chiefly joys in.

Ais.

I hear the beauty of this seat largely.

Ver.

It falls much short of that. *Exeunt. Manet* BEATRICE.

Bea.　　　　　　　　　　　　So, here's one step　　10
Into my father's favor; time will fix him.
I have got him now the liberty of the house:
So wisdom by degrees works out her freedom;
And if that eye be dark'ned that offends me—
I wait but that eclipse—this gentleman　　　　　15
Shall soon shine glorious in my father's liking,
Through the refulgent virtue of my love.

　　　　　　　　Enter DE FLORES.

De F.　　　　　　　　　　　　　　　　[*aside.*]

My thoughts are at a banquet; for the deed,
I feel no weight in't; 'tis but light and cheap
For the sweet recompense that I set down for't.　　20

Bea.

De Flores.

De F.　　　　　　　　Lady?

----

9. *I . . . largely*] I hear a great deal about . . .

10. *Exeunt.*] Evidently Jasperino goes to the rendezvous with Diaphanta during which they overhear part of this scene. See IV. ii. 89ff. and note.

　　one step] Alsemero's being shown over the castle by Vermandero.

11. *fix*] Make him a fixture.

14. *If . . . me*] If Alonzo be killed.

18. *for*] As for.

20. *For*] In exchange for.

　　set down] Enter, as in a mental account book.

Bea.   Thy looks promise cheerfully.
De F.

All things are answerable: time, circumstance,
Your wishes, and my service.

Bea.   Is it done, then?
De F.

Piracquo is no more.

Bea.

My joys start at mine eyes; our sweet'st delights   25
Are evermore born weeping.

De F.   I've a token for you.
Bea.

For me?

De F.

But it was sent somewhat unwillingly:
I could not get the ring without the finger.

                                        [*Shows her the finger.*]

Bea.

Bless me! What hast thou done?

De F.   Why is that more
Than killing the whole man? I cut his heartstrings.   30
A greedy hand thrust in a dish at court
In a mistake hath had as much as this.

Bea.

'Tis the first token my father made me send him.

De F.

And I made him send it back again
For his last token. I was loath to leave it,   35
And I'm sure dead men have no use of jewels.

---

21. *Thy . . . cheerfully*] You look as though you bring good
news.

32.] Has had a finger cut off accidentally by another diner's
knife.

33. *'Tis*] The ring is.

He was as loath to part with't, for it stuck
As if the flesh and it were both one substance.

Bea.

"At the stag's fall the keeper has his fees."
'Tis soon appli'd: all dead men's fees are yours, sir.   40
I pray, bury the finger, but the stone
You may make use on shortly; the true value,
Take't of my truth, is near three hundred ducats.

De F.

'Twill hardly buy a capcase for one's conscience, though,
To keep it from the worm, as fine as 'tis.   45
Well, being my fees, I'll take it;
Great men have taught me that, or else my merit
Would scorn the way on't.

Bea.   It might justly, sir—
Why, thou mistak'st, De Flores, 'tis not given
In state of recompense.

De F.   No, I hope so, lady;   50
You should soon witness my contempt to't then!

Bea.

Prithee, thou look'st as if thou wert offended.

De F.

That were strange, lady; 'tis not possible
My service should draw such a cause from you.
Offended? Could you think so? That were much   55
For one of my performance, and so warm
Yet in my service.

Bea.

'Twere misery in me to give you cause, sir.

---

42. *shortly*] Soon.
44. *capcase*] Casket.
50. *In state of*] As.
    so] We would say "not."
54. *cause*] Accusation.
58. *'Twere . . . cause*] I should be distressed to offend you.

De F.

    I know so much: it were so; misery
    In her most sharp condition.

Bea.   'Tis resolv'd, then;   60

    Look you, sir, here's three thousand golden florins:
    I have not meanly thought upon thy merit.

De F.

    What, salary! Now you move me.

Bea.   How, De Flores?

De F.

    Do you place me in the rank of verminous fellows
    To destroy things for wages? Offer gold?   65
    The lifeblood of man! Is anything
    Valued too precious for my recompense?

Bea.

    I understand thee not.

De F.   I could ha' hired

    A journeyman in murder at this rate
    And mine own conscience might have [slept at ease]   70
    And have had the work brought home.

Bea.   [*aside.*]

                    I'm in a labyrinth;
    What will content him? I would fain be rid of him.—
    I'll double the sum, sir.

De F.   You take a course

    To double my vexation, that's the good you do.

    59–60.] De Flores' reply is cryptic and bitterly ironical: "I know. It was the sharpest distress to me to offend *you.*"

    60. *'Tis resolv'd, then*] Beatrice misunderstands him: "Since you understand, your sense of injury is dissolved."

    63. *move me*] To anger.

    68–9. *I . . . rate*] At this wage scale I could have hired a killer.

    71. *brought home*] Accomplished easily.

Bea.   [*aside.*]
  Bless me! I am now in worse plight than I was;   75
  I know not what will please him.—For my fear's sake
  I prithee make away with all speed possible.
  And if thou be'st so modest not to name
  The sum that will content thee, paper blushes not;
  Send thy demand in writing; it shall follow thee.   80
  But prithee take thy flight.
De F.   You must fly too, then.
Bea.
  I?
De F.
  I'll not stir a foot else.
Bea.   What's your meaning?
De F.
  Why, are not you as guilty? In, I'm sure,
  As deep as I? And we should stick together.
  Come, your fears counsel you but ill: my absence   85
  Would draw suspect upon you instantly;
  There were no rescue for you.
Bea.   [*aside.*]
                                                       He speaks home.
De F.
  Nor is it fit we two, engag'd so jointly,
  Should part and live asunder.   [*Tries to kiss her.*]
Bea.   How now, sir?
  This shows not well.
De F.   What makes your lip so strange?   90
  This must not be betwixt us.
Bea.   [*aside.*]
                                                       The man talks wildly.

---

  87. *He speaks home*] He brings my guilt and danger home to
me.
  90. *What makes*] Why is.
  91. *This*] Strangeness.

De F.

    Come, kiss me with a zeal now.

Bea.   [*aside.*]

                          Heaven, I doubt him!

De F.

    I will not stand so long to beg 'em, shortly.

Bea.

    Take heed, De Flores, of forgetfulness;

    'Twill soon betray us.

De F.   Take you heed first;   95

    Faith, y'are grown much forgetful, y'are to blame in't.

Bea.   [*aside.*]

    He's bold, and I am blam'd for't!

De F.   I have eas'd you

    Of your trouble. Think on't! I'm in pain

    And must be eas'd of you; 'tis a charity.

    Justice invites your blood to understand me.   100

Bea.

    I dare not.

De F.   Quickly!

Bea.   O, I never shall!

    Speak it yet further off, that I may lose

    What has been spoken and no sound remain on't.

    I would not hear so much offense again

    For such another deed.

De F.   Soft, lady, soft!   105

    The last is not yet paid for. O, this act

    Has put me into spirit; I was as greedy on't

---

92. *doubt*] Fear.
93. *'em*] Kisses.
    shortly] Soon.
94. *forgetfulness*] Of my rank.
96. *forgetful*] Of your guilt, which is equal with mine.
99. *of*] By.
105. *Soft*] Not so fast!

As the parch'd earth of moisture when the clouds weep.
Did you not mark I wrought myself into't,
Nay, sued and kneel'd for't? Why was all that pains took?   110
You see I have thrown contempt upon your gold—
Not that I want it [not], for I do, piteously.
In order I will come unto't and make use on't;
But 'twas not held so precious to begin with,
For I place wealth after the heels of pleasure   115
And were I not resolv'd in my belief
That thy virginity were perfect in thee
I should but take my recompense with grudging,
As if I had but half my hopes I agreed for.
Bea.
Why, 'tis impossible thou canst be so wicked   120
Or shelter such a cunning cruelty
To make his death the murderer of my honor.
Thy language is so bold and vicious
I cannot see which way I can forgive it
With any modesty.
De F.   Push! You forget yourself.   125
A woman dipp'd in blood, and talk of modesty!
Bea.
O misery of sin! Would I had been bound
Perpetually unto my living hate
In that Piracquo than to hear these words.
Think but upon the distance that creation   130
Set 'twixt thy blood and mine, and keep thee there.
De F.
Look but into your conscience, read me there;
'Tis a true book; you'll find me there your equal.
Push! Fly not to your birth, but settle you

---

113. *In order*] In due course.
122. *To*] As to.
129. *than*] Rather than.
131. *keep thee there*] Stay in your place.

In what the act has made you; y'are no more now.   135
You must forget your parentage to me:
Y'are the deed's creature; by that name
You lost your first condition, and I challenge you
As peace and innocency has turn'd you out
And made you one with me.

Bea.   With thee, foul villain?   140

De F.

Yes, my fair murd'ress. Do you urge me?
Though thou writ'st maid, thou whore in thy affection,
'Twas chang'd from thy first love, and that's a kind
Of whoredom in thy heart. And he's chang'd now
To bring thy second on, thy Alsemero,   145
Whom, by all sweets that ever darkness tasted,
If I enjoy thee not, thou ne'er enjoy'st!
I'll blast the hopes and joys of marriage,
I'll confess all; my life I rate at nothing.

Bea.

De Flores!   150

De F.

I shall rest from all lovers' plagues then;
I live in pain now: that shooting eye
Will burn my heart to cinders.

Bea.   O, sir, hear me.

De F.

She that in life and love refuses me,
In death and shame my partner she shall be.   155

---

136. *to me*] In your relation with me (Brooke); perhaps (You must forget) the eminence of your birth compared with mine.

138. *first condition*] Innocence.

138–40. *I . . . you/ As*] I claim equality with you/ On the ground that.

141. *urge*] Provoke me into using plainer words.

143. *'Twas*] Your affection was.

144. *chang'd*] Dead—another changeling!

Bea.

    Stay, hear me once for all: [*kneels*] I make thee master
    Of all the wealth I have in gold and jewels.
    Let me go poor unto my bed with honor
    And I am rich in all things.

De F.   Let this silence thee:

    The wealth of all Valencia shall not buy   160
    My pleasure from me.
    Can you weep fate from its determin'd purpose?
    So soon may [you] weep me.

Bea.   Vengeance begins;

    Murder, I see, is followed by more sins.
    Was my creation in the womb so curs'd   165
    It must engender with a viper first?

De F.

    Come, rise, and shroud your blushes in my bosom;
                       [*Raises her.*]
    Silence is one of pleasure's best receipts:
    Thy peace is wrought forever in this yielding.
    'Las, how the turtle pants! Thou'lt love anon   170
    What thou so fear'st and faint'st to venture on. *Exeunt.*

---

168. *of . . . receipts*] Of the best recipes for sexual enjoyment.
170. *turtle*] Turtledove.
    anon] At once.

Beatrice

ACTUS QUARTUS

[IV.i]

[Dumb Show.]

Enter Gentlemen, VERMANDERO *meeting them with action of wonderment at the flight of* PIRACQUO. *Enter* ALSEMERO *with* JASPERINO, *and Gallants.* VERMANDERO *points to him, the Gentlemen seeming to applaud the choice.* [*Exeunt in procession*] ALSEMERO, JASPERINO, *and Gentlemen,* BEATRICE, *the bride, following in great state, accompanied with* DIAPHANTA, ISABELLA, *and other Gentlewomen.* DE FLORES *after all, smiling at the accident.* ALONZO'S *ghost appears to* DE FLORES *in the midst of his smile, startles him, showing him the hand whose finger he had cut off. They pass over in great solemnity.*

Enter BEATRICE.

Bea.
This fellow has undone me endlessly;
Never was bride so fearfully distress'd.
The more I think upon th'ensuing night,
And whom I am to cope with in embraces,

IV.i.] Alsemero's Apartment in the Castle.
0.9. *accident*] Incident.

One that's ennobled both in blood and mind,   5
So clear in understanding—that's my plague now—
Before whose judgment will my fault appear
Like malefactors' crimes before tribunals—
There is no hiding on't—the more I dive
Into my own distress. How a wise man   10
Stands for a great calamity! There's no venturing
Into his bed, what course soe'er I light upon,
Without my shame, which may grow up to danger;
He cannot but in justice strangle me
As I lie by him, as a cheater use me.   15
'Tis a precious craft to play with a false die
Before a cunning gamester. Here's his closet,
The key left in't, and he abroad i' th' park.
Sure, 'twas forgot; I'll be so bold as look in't.
                                         [*Opens closet.*]
Bless me! A right physician's closet 'tis,   20
Set round with vials; every one her mark, too.
Sure, he does practice physic for his own use,
Which may be safely call'd your great man's wisdom.
What manuscript lies here? "The Book of Experiment,
Call'd Secrets in Nature." So 'tis, 'tis so.   25
"How to know whether a woman be with child or no."
I hope I am not yet. If he should try, though!
Let me see: "Folio forty-five." Here 'tis,
The leaf tuck'd down upon't, the place suspicious.
"If you would know whether a woman be with child or   30

---

11. *stands for*] May represent.
16. *'Tis . . . craft*] It needs rare skill.
     die] One of a pair of dice.
20. *right*] Regular.
27. *Secrets of Nature*] A book with this title *(De arcanis naturae)* was published by the Antonius Mizaldus (1520–1578) mentioned in 1. 46. It contains no tests of virginity, but another work of the same author does, though not those described here.

not, give her two spoonfuls of the white water in glass
C—"
Where's that glass C? O, yonder, I see't now—
"and if she be with child, she sleeps full twelve hours
after; if not, not."   35
None of that water comes into my belly.
I'll know you from a hundred; I could break you now
Or turn you into milk, and so beguile
The master of the mystery; but I'll look to you.
Ha! That which is next is ten times worse: 40
"How to know whether a woman be a maid or not."
If that should be appli'd, what would become of me?
Belike he has a strong faith of my purity
That never yet made proof. But this he calls
"A merry sleight, but true experiment, the author   45
Antonius Mizaldus. Give the party you suspect the
quantity of a spoonful of the water in the glass M,
which upon her that is a maid makes three several
effects: 'twill make her incontinently gape, then fall
into a sudden sneezing, last into a violent laughing;
else, dull, heavy, and lumpish."   50
Where had I been?
I fear it. Yet 'tis seven hours to bedtime.
                    Enter DIAPHANTA.
Dia.
Cuds, madam, are you here?

---

37. *You . . . you*] Glass C.
38. *turn . . . milk*] Replace your contents with milk.
39. *look to you*] Get round you somehow.
48. *incontinently*] Immediately.
50. *heavy*] Sluggish.
51.] I.e. if he had tested me.
52. *Yet . . . bedtime*] I still have seven hours in which to
think of some device.
53. *Cuds*] Ye gods!

Bea.   [*aside.*]
                    Seeing that wench now,
  A trick comes in my mind: 'tis a nice piece
  Gold cannot purchase.—I come hither, wench,   55
  To look my lord.
Dia.   [*aside.*]
  Would I had such a cause to look him, too!—
  Why, he's i' th' park, madam.
Bea.
  There let him be.
Dia.   Ay, madam, let him compass
  Whole parks and forests, as great rangers do,   60
  At roosting time a little lodge can hold 'em.
  Earth-conquering Alexander, that thought the world
  Too narrow for him, in the end had but his pit-hole.
Bea.
  I fear thou art not modest, Diaphanta.
Dia.
  Your thoughts are so unwilling to be known, madam;   65
  'Tis ever the bride's fashion towards bedtime
  To set light by her joys as if she ow'd 'em not.
Bea.
  Her joys? Her fears, thou would'st say.
Dia.   Fear of what?
Bea.
  Art thou a maid, and talk'st so to a maid?

54–5. *'tis . . . purchase*] It's a scrupulous specimen of humanity whom gold cannot bribe.

60. *rangers*] Gamekeepers.

63. *pit-hole*] Grave; but ll. 64–7 suggest a bawdy double meaning.

67. *set light by*] Make light of.
    ow'd] Owned.

You leave a blushing business behind,   70
  Beshrew your heart for't.
Dia.   Do you mean good sooth, madam?
Bea.
  Well, if I'd thought upon the fear at first,
  Man should have been unknown.
Dia.   Is't possible?
Bea.
  I will give a thousand ducats to that woman
  Would try what my fear were, and tell me true   75
  Tomorrow when she gets from't. As she likes,
  I might perhaps be drawn to't.
Dia.   Are you in earnest?
Bea.
  Do you get the woman, then challenge me
  And see if I'll fly from't. But I must tell you
  This by the way: she must be a true maid,   80
  Else there's no trial; my fears are not hers, else.
Dia.
  Nay, she that I would put into your hands, madam,
  Shall be a maid.
Bea.   You know I should be sham'd else,
  Because she lies for me.
Dia.   'Tis a strange humor.
  But are you serious still? Would you resign   85
  Your first night's pleasure, and give money, too?
Bea.
  As willingly as live. [*Aside.*] Alas, the gold

    70–1. *You . . . for't*] You leave me blushing, confound you!
    71. *Do . . . sooth*] Are you in earnest? (Cf. l. 77, below).
    78–9. *Do . . . from't*] You get the woman, then make your demand, and see if I'll renege.
    84. *lies for*] A common pun.
         humor] Whim.

Is but a by-bet to wedge in the honor.
Dia.   [*aside.*]
I do not know how the world goes abroad
For faith or honesty; there's both requir'd in this.—   90
Madam, what say you to me, and stray no further?
I've a good mind, in troth, to earn your money.
Bea.
Y'are too quick, I fear, to be a maid.
Dia.
How? Not a maid? Nay, then you urge me, madam;
Your honorable self is not a truer   95
With all your fears upon you—
Bea.   [*aside.*]
                                                   Bad enough, then.
Dia.
Than I with all my lightsome joys about me.
Bea.
I'm glad to hear't; then you dare put your honesty
Upon an easy trial?
Dia.   Easy? Anything!
Bea.
I'll come to you straight.   [*Goes to the closet.*]
Dia.   [*aside.*]
                              She will not search me, will she,
Like the forewoman of a female jury?   101
Bea.
Glass M. Ay, this is it. Look. Diaphanta,
You take no worse than I do.   [*Drinks.*]
Dia.   And in so doing
I will not question what 'tis, but take it.   [*Drinks.*]

---

88. *by-bet . . . honor*] Hedge to make sure of the main
risk, my reputation.

90. *For*] As to.

94. *urge*] Cf. III.iv.141n.

98. *honesty*] Virginity.

Bea.   [*aside.*]
Now, if the experiment be true, 'twill praise itself
And give me noble ease. Begins already!   106
                              [DIAPHANTA *gapes.*]
There's the first symptom; and what haste it makes
To fall into the second, there by this time!
                              [DIAPHANTA *sneezes.*]
Most admirable secret! On the contrary,
It stirs not me a whit, which most concerns it.   110
Dia.
Ha, ha, ha!
Bea.   [*aside.*]
                              Just in all things and in order
As if 'twere circumscrib'd: one accident
Gives way unto another.
Dia.   Ha, ha, ha!
Bea.   How now, wench?
Dia.
Ha, ha, ha! I am so, so light at heart, ha, ha, ha, so
pleasurable.
But one swig more, sweet madam.
Bea.   Ay, tomorrow;   115
We shall have time to sit by't.
Dia.   Now I'm sad again.

---

105. *praise itself*] (Ap)praise itself, show its value.

110. *which . . . it*] Which is its most important function,
since I am no longer a virgin.

112. *circumscrib'd*] Specific in its effects.
       accident] Symptom.

115–16. *Ay . . . by't*] Beatrice is anxious to get away from
Alsemero's apartment, where a fiancée's presence is unconven-
tional. Tomorrow she will belong there as his wife, and she and
Diaphanta will be able to drink the "water" at their leisure.

Bea.   [*aside.*]

It lays itself so gently, too.—Come, wench;
Most honest Diaphanta I dare call thee now.

Dia.

Pray tell me, madam, what trick call you this?

Bea.

I'll tell thee all hereafter; we must study   120
The carriage of this business.

Dia.   I shall carry't well

Because I love the burden.

Bea.   About midnight

You must not fail to steal forth gently,
That I may use the place.

Dia.   O, fear not, madam,

I shall be cool by that time. [*Aside.*] The bride's place,   125
And with a thousand ducats! I'm for a justice now:
I bring a portion with me; I scorn small fools. *Exeunt.*

[IV.ii]

Enter VERMANDERO *and Servant.*

Ver.

I tell thee, knave, mine honor is in question,
A thing till now free from suspicion,
Nor ever was there cause. Who of my gentlemen
Are absent? Tell me, and truly, how many and who.

Ser.

Antonio, sir, and Franciscus.   5

---

117. *lays itself*] Subsides.
118. *honest*] Virginal.
121. *carriage*] Handling.
126–7.] With a thousand ducats, I'm for a big fool, a justice
(Spencer). Cf. I.ii.125–30.
IV.ii.] Another Apartment in the Castle.

Ver.

When did they leave the castle?

Ser.

Some ten days since, sir, the one intending to Briamata, th'other for Valencia.

Ver.

The time accuses 'em. A charge of murder
Is brought within my castle gate, Piracquo's murder;   10
I dare not answer faithfully their absence.
A strict command of apprehension
Shall pursue 'em suddenly, and either wipe
The stain off clear or openly discover it.
Provide me wingèd warrants for the purpose.

                                        Exit Servant.   15

See, I am set on again.

                        Enter TOMAZO.

Tom.

I claim a brother of you.

Ver.   Y'are too hot;
Seek him not here.

Tom.   Yes, 'mongst your dearest bloods,
If my peace find no fairer satisfaction;
This is the place must yield account for him,   20
For here I left him; and the hasty tie
Of this snatch'd marriage gives strong testimony
Of his most certain ruin.

Ver.   Certain falsehood!
This is the place indeed; his breach of faith

---

7. *Briamata*] Vermandero's country house.
11. *answer faithfully*] Explain with confidence.
16. *set on*] Harassed.
18. *bloods*] Relatives.
22. *snatch'd*] Hasty.
24. *breach of faith*] Desertion.

Has too much marr'd both my abusèd love,   25
The honorable love I reserv'd for him,
And mock'd my daughter's joy; the prepar'd morning
Blush'd at his infidelity; he left
Contempt and scorn to throw upon those friends
Whose belief hurt 'em. O, 'twas most ignoble   30
To take his flight so unexpectedly
And throw such public wrongs on those that lov'd him.

Tom.

Then this is all your answer?

Ver.   'Tis too fair

For one of his alliance; and I warn you
That this place no more see you.   *Exit.*

                        Enter DE FLORES.

Tom.   [*aside.*]
                                        The best is,   35
There is more ground to meet a man's revenge on.—
Honest De Flores!

De F.   That's my name, indeed.

Saw you the bride? Good, sweet sir, which way took she?

Tom.

I have blest mine eyes from seeing such a false one.

De F.   [*aside.*]

I'd fain get off; this man's not for my company;   40
I smell his brother's blood when I come near him.

Tom.

Come hither, kind and true one; I remember
My brother lov'd thee well.

De F.   O, purely, dear sir.

[*Aside.*] Methinks I am now again a-killing on him,
He brings it so fresh to me.

---

34. *one of his alliance*] Anyone connected with him.

36.] There is another way to find out whom I must take vengeance on.

Tom.   Thou canst guess, sirrah—   45
   One honest friend has an instinct of jealousy—
   At some foul guilty person.
De F.
   'Las, sir, I am so charitable, I think none worse than
   myself.—You did not see the bride, then?
Tom.
   I prithee, name her not. Is she not wicked?   50
De F.
   No, no; a pretty, easy, round-pack'd sinner,
   As your most ladies are, else you might think
   I flatter'd her; but, sir, at no hand wicked
   Till th'are so old their chins and noses meet,
   And they salute witches.—I am call'd, I think, sir.   55
   [*Aside.*] His company ev'n o'erlays my conscience. *Exit.*
Tom.
   That De Flores has a wondrous honest heart:
   He'll bring it out in time, I'm assur'd on't.
   O, here's the glorious master of the day's joy.
   'Twill not be long till he and I do reckon.   60
                 Enter ALSEMERO.
   Sir!
Als.
   You are most welcome.

---

   46. *One*] The suggestion is that De Flores is Tomazo's only
honest friend among a group of deceivers and enemies; but
Tomazo may be flattering De Flores to gain information. Cf.
V.ii.1–43.
     jealousy] Suspicion.
   51. *round-pack'd*] Plump.
   53. *at no hand*] By no means.
   55. *salute*] Greet, consort with.
   56. *o'erlays my conscience*] Oppresses my thoughts.
   58. *bring it out*] Come out with the name of the suspect.
   59. *glorious*] Vainglorious.

Tom.   You may call that word back;
I do not think I am, nor wish to be.
Als.
'Tis strange you found the way to this house, then.
Tom.
Would I'd ne'er known the cause! I'm none of those, sir,   65
That come to give you joy and swill your wine;
'Tis a more precious liquor that must lay
The fiery thirst I bring.
Als.   Your words and you
Appear to me great strangers.
Tom.   Time and our swords
May make us more acquainted. This the business: 70
I should have a brother in your place;
How treachery and malice have dispos'd of him
I'm bound to inquire of him which holds his right,
Which never could come fairly.
Als.   You must look
To answer for that word, sir.
Tom.   Fear you not,   75
I'll have it ready drawn at our next meeting.
Keep your day solemn. Farewell, I disturb it not;
I'll bear the smart with patience for a time.   *Exit.*
Als.
'Tis somewhat ominous, this: a quarrel ent'red
Upon this day! My innocence relieves me;   80

---

65. *cause*] Reason for coming.
67. *liquor*] Blood.
   lay] Quell. Cf. IV.i.117.
73. *him . . . right*] Alsemero, who has Alonzo's promised bride and dowry.
76. *it ready drawn*] 1) My answer drawn up; 2) my sword drawn.
77. *Keep . . . solemn*] Proceed with the wedding solemnities.

Enter JASPERINO.

I should be wondrous sad, else.—Jasperino,
I have news to tell thee, strange news.

Jas.   I ha' some, too,
I think as strange as yours; would I might keep
Mine, so my faith and friendship might be kept in't!
Faith, sir, dispense a little with my zeal   85
And let it cool in this.

Als.   This puts me on
And blames thee for thy slowness.

Jas.   All may prove nothing;
Only a friendly fear that leapt from me, sir.

Als.

No question it may prove nothing; let's partake it, though.

Jas.

'Twas Diaphanta's chance—for to that wench   90
I pretend honest love and she deserves it—
To leave me in a back part of the house,
A place we chose for private conference;
She was no sooner gone but instantly
I heard your bride's voice in the next room to me;   95
And, lending more attention, found De Flores
Louder than she.

Als.   De Flores? Thou art out now.

Jas.

You'll tell me more anon.

Als.   Still I'll prevent thee:
The very sight of him is poison to her.

---

84. *so*] Provided that.
85. *dispense . . . with*] Forgo somewhat.
86. *puts me on*] Increases my eagerness.
91. *pretend*] Offer.
97. *out*] Wrong.
98. *You'll . . . more*] Cf. III.i.5n.
    prevent thee] Avert your error.

Jas.

That made me stagger, too, but Diaphanta   100
At her return confirm'd it.

Als.   Diaphanta!

Jas.

Then fell we both to listen, and words pass'd
Like those that challenge interest in a woman.

Als.

Peace, quench thy zeal; 'tis dangerous to thy bosom.

Jas.

Then truth is full of peril.

Als.   Such truths are.   105
O, were she the sole glory of the earth,
Had eyes that could shoot fire into kings' breasts,
And touch'd, she sleeps not here! Yet I have time,
Though night be near, to be resolv'd hereof;
And prithee do not weigh me by my passions.   110

Isa.

I never weigh'd friend so.

Als.   Done charitably!
That key will lead thee to a pretty secret   [*Gives key.*]
By a Chaldean taught me, and I've
My study upon some. Bring from my closet
A glass inscrib'd there with the letter M,   115
And question not my purpose.

100–1. *That . . . it*] That belief made me doubt my own
ears, too, but Diaphanta confirmed that it was De Flores with
Beatrice.

103. *challenge*] Call forth.

108. *touch'd*] Tainted.

109. *resolv'd*] Convinc'd one way or the other.

110. *passions*] Outbursts of passion.

113. *Chaldean*] Astrologer (*Daniel* ii.2).

113–14. *I've . . . some*] I'm doing research on some other
secrets.

Jas.   It shall be done, sir.   [*Exit.*]

Als.

How can this hang together? Not an hour since,
Her woman came pleading her lady's fears,
Deliver'd her for the most timorous virgin
That ever shrunk at man's name, and so modest   120
She charg'd her weep out her request to me
That she might come obscurely to my bosom.

                 Enter BEATRICE.

Bea.   [*aside.*]

All things go well; my woman's preparing yonder
For her sweet voyage, which grieves me to lose.
Necessity compels it: I lose all, else.   125

Als.   [*aside.*]

Push! Modesty's shrine is set in yonder forehead.
I cannot be too sure, though.—My Joanna!

Bea.

Sir, I was bold to weep a message to you.
Pardon my modest fears.

Als.   [*aside.*]

                    The dove's not meeker.
She's abus'd, questionless.—

             Reenter JASPERINO [*with glass*].

                      O, are you come, sir?   130

Bea   [*aside.*]

The glass, upon my life! I see the letter.

Jas.

Sir, this is M.

Als.   'Tis it.

---

117. *since*] Ago.
119. *Deliver'd her for*] Described her as.
121–2. *She . . . her . . . her . . . she*] Beatrice . . . Diaphanta
. . . Beatrice's . . . Beatrice.
122. *obscurely*] In the dark.

Bea.   [*aside.*]
                                        I am suspected.

Als.

How fitly our bride comes to partake with us!

Bea.

What is't, my lord?

Als.

                              No hurt.

Bea.   Sir, pardon me,
I seldom taste of any composition.   135

Als.

But this upon my warrant you shall venture on.

Bea.

I fear 'twill make me ill.

Als.   Heaven forbid that!

Bea.   [*aside.*]
I'm put now to my cunning: th' effects I know,
If I can now but feign 'em handsomely.   [*Drinks.*]

Als.

It has that secret virtue, it ne'er miss'd, sir,   140
Upon a virgin.

Jas.   Treble qualitied?
                    [BEATRICE *gapes, then sneezes.*]

Als.

By all that's virtuous, it takes there, proceeds!

---

135. *composition*] Mixture.

140–1. *it . . . virgin*] That it has never failed to detect a
virgin.

141. *Treble qualitied?*] This may be either a query or an
observation, either on the high quality of the virginity or the
high efficacy of the potion; or it may refer to the threefold effect,
though we do not know that Jasperino has been told of that.

141.lff.] Beatrice is cleverly made to echo some of Diaphanta's
words (cf. IV.i.114 and l. 145) as well as to imitate her actions.

Jas.

This is the strangest trick to know a maid by.

Bea.

Ha, ha, ha!

You have given me joy of heart to drink, my lord.   145

Als.

No, thou hast given me such joy of heart

That never can be blasted.

Bea.   What's the matter, sir?

Als.   [*aside.*]

See, now 'tis settled in a melancholy;

Keeps both the time and method.—My Joanna!

Chaste as the breath of heaven or morning's womb   150

That brings the day forth, thus my love encloses thee.

                              [*Embraces her.*] *Exeunt.*

[IV.iii]

                    Enter ISABELLA *and* LOLLIO.

Isa.

O, heaven! Is this the waiting moon?

Does love turn fool, run mad, and all [at] once?

Sirrah, here's a madman, akin to the fool, too,

A lunatic lover.

Lol.

No, no, not he I brought the letter from?   5

Isa.

Compare his inside with his out and tell me.

                    [*Gives him the letter.*]

Lol.

The out's mad, I'm sure of that; I had a taste on't.

---

147. *That*] As.

IV.iii.] A Room in Alibius' House.

1. *waiting*] Lying in wait, ominous. Cf. V.iii.196–7.

6. *inside . . . out*] Contents . . . superscription.

   his] Its.

[*Reads.*] "To the bright Andromeda, chief chambermaid
to the Knight of the Sun, at the sign of Scorpio, in the
Middle Region, sent by the bellows-mender of Aeolus.   10
Pay the post." This is stark madness.

Isa.

Now mark the inside. [*Takes the letter and reads.*]
"Sweet lady, having now cast off this counterfeit cover
of a madman, I appear to your best judgment a true
and faithful lover of your beauty."

Lol.

He is mad still.

Isa.

"If any fault you find, chide those perfections in you
which have made me imperfect. 'Tis the same sun that
causeth to grow and enforceth to wither—"

Lol.

O, rogue!

Isa.

"shapes and transshapes, destroys and builds again. I
come in winter to you dismantled of my proper ornaments; by the sweet splendor of your cheerful smiles, I
spring and live a lover."

Lol.

Mad rascal still!   25

8–11.] Not, as Lollio (l. 11) calls it, "stark madness." There
are touches of method that remind us that Franciscus is pretending. Andromeda-Isabella is to be rescued by Perseus-Franciscus
from the dragon (Alibius); chambermaids were thought to be
lascivious (V.i.16ff.), and read old romances like *The Mirror of
Knighthood*, in which the Knight of the Sun is among the heroes;
Scorpio is the sign of the zodiac governing the privates (Middle
Region); Aeolus, god of the winds, might well need a bellows-
mender.

10. *Middle Region*] The fifth to eighth months of the astro-
logical year.

Isa.

"Tread him not under foot, that shall appear an honor
to your bounties. I remain—mad till I speak with you,
from whom I expect my cure. Yours all, or one beside
himself, FRANCISCUS."

Lol.

You are like to have a fine time on't. My master and I   30
may give over our professions: I do not think but you
can cure fools and madmen faster than we, with little
pains, too.

Isa.

Very likely.

Lol.

One thing I must tell you, mistress: you perceive that I
am privy to your skill. If I find you minister once and   35
set up the trade, I put in for my thirds; I shall be mad
or fool else.

Isa.

The first place is thine, believe it, Lollio;
If I do fall—

Lol.

I fall upon you.   40

Isa.

So.

Lol.

Well, I stand to my venture.

Isa.

But thy counsel, now: how shall I deal with 'em?

Lol.

Why, do you mean to deal with 'em?

---

36. *my thirds*] My one-third share. The other two-thirds went
to the king.

42. *venture*] His application for *thirds* (l. 36).

Isa.

Nay, the fair understanding: how to use 'em.   45

Lol.

Ab-use 'em! That's the way to mad the fool and make a
fool of the madman, and then you use 'em kindly.

Isa.

'Tis easy; I'll practice, do thou observe it.
The key of thy wardrobe.

Lol.

There. Fit yourself for 'em and I'll fit 'em both for you.   50
                                              [*Gives her the key.*]

Isa.

Take thou no further notice than the outside.   *Exit.*

Lol.

Not an inch; I'll put you to the inside.
                              Enter ALIBIUS.

Alib.

Lollio, art there? Will all be perfect, think'st thou?
Tomorrow night, as if to close up the solemnity,
Vermandero expects us.   55

Lol.

I mistrust the madmen most; the fools will do well
enough: I have taken pains with them.

Alib.

Tush! They cannot miss: the more absurdity,
The more commends it, so no rough behaviors

---

45. *fair understanding*] Decent meaning.
        use] Treat.
47. *kindly*] 1) After their kind; 2) considerately.
50. *fit . . . fit*] Dress . . . prepare.
51.] Don't betray me in my mad garb. Cf. l. 6, above.
52. *I'll . . . inside*] I'll leave the proposed love-making to
you.
59. *so*] Provided that.

Affright the ladies; they are nice things, thou know'st.   60
Lol.

You need not fear, sir; so long as we are there with our
commanding pizzles, they'll be as tame as the ladies
themselves.
Alib.

I will see them once more rehearse before they go.
Lol.

I was about it, sir; look you to the madmen's morris   65
and let me alone with the other. There is one or two
that I mistrust their fooling; I'll instruct them, and then
they shall rehearse the whole measure.
Alib.

Do so; I'll see the music prepar'd. But, Lollio,
By the way, how does my wife brook her restraint?   70
Does she not grudge at it?
Lol.

So-so; she takes some pleasure in the house; she would
abroad, else. You must allow her a little more length;
she's kept too short.
Alib.

She shall along to Vermandero's with us;   75
That will serve her for a month's liberty.
Lol.

What's that on your face, sir?
Alib.

Where, Lollio? I see nothing.

---

60. *nice things*] Fastidious creatures.
62. *pizzles*] Bulls' penises used as whips.
65. *morris*] Dance.
66. *let me alone*] Trust me.
66–7. *one or two . . . fooling*] Antonio and Franciscus.
70. *brook*] "Take."

Lol.

Cry you mercy, sir, 'tis your nose; it show'd like the
trunk of a young elephant.   80

Alib.

Away, rascal! I'll prepare the music, Lollio.

Lol.

Do, sir, and I'll dance the whilst. *Exit* ALIBIUS.
Tony, where art thou, Tony?

Enter ANTONIO.

Ant.

Here, cousin; where art thou?

Lol.

Come, Tony, the footmanship I taught you.   85

Ant.

I had rather ride, cousin.

Lol.

Ay, a whip take you! But I'll keep you out. Vault in:
look you, Tony: fa, la la la la.   [*Dances.*]

Ant.

Fa, la la la la.   [*Dances.*]

Lol.

There, an honor.   90

Ant.

Is this an honor, coz?

---

79. *Cry you mercy*] Pardon me.

79–80. *it . . . elephant*] I.e. from being led around by it
(Spencer); cuckolded.

85. *footmanship*] Skill in dancing.

86. *ride*] Cf. l. 151, below.

87. *out*] From riding.

Vault in] Jump into the dance.

90. *honor*] Bow.

91–9.] Antonio burlesques Lollio's movements.

Lol.

Yes, an it please your worship.

Ant.

Does honor bend in the hams, coz?

Lol.

Marry does it; as low as worship, squireship, nay,
yeomanry itself sometimes, from whence it first stiffened.   95
There, rise. A caper!

Ant.

Caper after an honor, coz?

Lol.

Very proper; for honor is but a caper, rises as fast and
high, has a knee or two, and falls to th' ground again.
You can remember your figure, Tony?   *Exit.*   100

Ant.

Yes, cousin, when I see thy figure, I can remember mine.

     Enter ISABELLA [like a madwoman].

Isa.

Hey, how he treads the air! Shoo, shoo, t'other way! He
burns his wings, else. Here's wax enough below, Icarus,
more than will be canceled these eighteen moons;
He's down, he's down! What a terrible fall he had!   105
Stand up, thou son of Cretan Dedalus,

---

92. *an*] If.

93. *hams*] Here, the knees.

94. *Marry does it*] By Mary, it does.

95. *stiffened*] Stood up straight.

99. *has . . . two*] Is curtsied to once or twice.

100–1. *your figure . . . thy figure*] 1) Dance; 2) you.

102–30.] For the "mad" talk, see the note on ll. 8–11, above.

103. *wax . . . canceled*] Wax melted from Icarus' wings,
and waxen seals on legal documents.

106–8.] Antonio-Icarus now becomes Theseus, to whom Isa-
bella-Ariadne gave the thread (*clue*) which led him out of the
labyrinth after killing the Minotaur (Alibius).

And let us tread the lower labyrinth;
I'll bring thee to the clue.
Ant.
Prithee, coz, let me alone.
Isa.
Art thou not drown'd?   110
About thy head I saw a heap of clouds
Wrapp'd like a Turkish turban; on thy back
A crook'd, chameleon-color'd rainbow hung
Like a tiara down unto thy hams.
Let me suck out those billows in thy belly;   115
Hark, how they roar and rumble in the straits!
Bless thee from the pirates.
Ant.
Pox upon you, let me alone!
Isa.
Why shouldst thou mount so high as Mercury
Unless thou hadst reversion of his place?   120
Stay in the moon with me, Endymion,
And we will rule these wild, rebellious waves
That would have drown'd my love.
Ant.
I'll kick thee if again thou touch me,

109, 118, 124.] Antonio becomes increasingly annoyed.

110.] Isabella reverts to the legend of Icarus, who was drowned.

114. *tiara*] Turban. Isabella seems to have in mind also a hip-length cloak, perhaps attached to the turban at the back.

116. *straits*] Here, intestines.

116–17.] Many straits in the Mediterranean were notorious as pirate lairs.

120. *reversion of*] Right to succeed to.

122–3.] Perhaps the legend of Hero and Leander enters the confusion.

Thou wild, unshapen antic; I am no fool,   125
You bedlam!
Isa.   But you are, as sure as I am, mad.
Have I put on this habit of a frantic,
With love as full of fury to beguile
The nimble eye of watchful jealousy,
And am I thus rewarded?   [*Reveals herself.*]
Ant.
Ha! Dearest beauty!   131
Isa.   No, I have no beauty now,
Nor never had but what was in my garments.
You a quick-sighted lover? Come not near me!
Keep your caparisons, y'are aptly clad;
I came a feigner to return stark mad.   *Exit.*   135
Ant.
Stay, or I shall change condition
And become as you are.   *Reenter* LOLLIO.
Lol.
Why, Tony, whither now? Why, fool—
Ant.
Whose fool, usher of idiots? You coxcomb!
I have fool'd too much.   140
Lol.
You were best be mad another while, then.
Ant.
So I am, stark mad; I have cause enough,
And I could throw the full effects on thee
And beat thee like a fury.
Lol.
Do not, do not; I shall not forbear the gentleman under   145

---

125. *antic*] Buffoon.

126. *bedlam*] Here, lunatic.

134.] Retain your trappings; you really are a fool.

145–6. *I . . . fool*] I'll not submit to the fool's attack just
because he is a gentleman in disguise.

the fool if you do. Alas, I saw through your fox-skin
before now. Come, I can give you comfort: my mistress
loves you, and there is as arrant a madman i' th' house
as you are a fool—your rival, whom she loves not. If
after the masque we can rid her of him, you earn her   150
love, she says, and the fool shall ride her.

Ant.

May I believe thee?

Lol.

Yes, or you may choose whether you will or no.

Ant.

She's eas'd of him; I have a good quarrel on't.

Lol.

Well, keep your old station yet, and be quiet.   155

Ant.

Tell her I will deserve her love.   *Exit.*

Lol.

And you are like to have your desire.

Enter FRANCISCUS.

Fran.   [*sings.*]

"Down, down, down a-down, a-down"—and then with
a horse-trick to kick Latona's forehead and break her
bowstring.

Lol.   [*aside.*]

This is t'other counterfeit; I'll put him out of his humor.   160
[*Takes out letter and reads.*] "Sweet lady, having now

---

146. *fox-skin*] Clever disguise.

148. *madman*] Franciscus.

151. *fool*] Antonio.

154. *She's eas'd*] She shall be rid.

   I . . . on't] I have good reason to quarrel with him.

155. *station*] Status of fool.

158. *horse-trick*] Caper.

158–9.] More confusion; Diana with her bow seems to be
meant.

cast off this counterfeit cover of a madman, I appear to
your best judgment a true and faithful lover of your
beauty." This is pretty well for a madman.

Fran.

Ha! What's that?   165

Lol.

"Chide those perfections in you, which have made me
imperfect."

Fran.

I am discover'd to the fool.

Lol.

I hope to discover the fool in you ere I have done with
you. "Yours all, or one beside himself, FRANCISCUS."   170
This madman will mend, sure.

Fran.

What do you read, sirrah?

Lol.

Your destiny, sir: you'll be hang'd for this trick and
another that I know.

Fran.

Art thou of counsel with thy mistress?   175

Lol.

Next her apron strings.

Fran.

Give me thy hand.

Lol.

Stay, let me put yours in my pocket first. [*Puts away the
letter.*] Your hand is true, is it not? It will not pick?
I partly fear it, because I think it does lie.   180

Fran.

Not in a syllable.

168–9. *discover'd to . . . discover*] Found out by . . . find.
177–9. *hand . . . yours . . . hand*] 1) Hand; 2) handwriting.
179. *true*] Honest.
     pick] I.e. my pocket.

Lol.

So; if you love my mistress so well as you have handled
the matter here, you are like to be cur'd of your madness.

Fran.

And none but she can cure it.

Lol.

Well, I'll give you over, then, and she shall cast your   185
water next.

Fran.

Take for thy pains past.   [*Gives him money.*]

Lol.

I shall deserve more, sir, I hope; my mistress loves you,
but must have some proof of your love to her.

Fran.

There I meet my wishes.   190

Lol.

That will not serve; you must meet her enemy and yours.

Fran.

He's dead already.

Lol.

Will you tell me that, and I parted but now with him?

Fran.

Show me the man.

Lol.

Ay, that's a right course, now; see him before you kill   195
him in any case. And yet it needs not go so far, neither;
'tis but a fool that haunts the house and my mistress in
the shape of an idiot; bang but his fool's coat well-
favoredly and 'tis well.

---

183. *here*] In the letter.
185–6. *she . . . next*] Diagnose your malady by urinalysis.
192. *dead*] As good as dead.
198–200. *well-favoredly . . . Soundly*] *Soundly* explains both
the severity of the banging and the soundness of Lollio's advice.

Fran.

Soundly, soundly.   200

Lol.

Only reserve him till the masque be past, and if you
find him not now in the dance yourself, I'll show you.
In, in! My master!

Fran.

He handles him like a feather. Hey!   [*Exit dancing.*]
                              Enter ALIBIUS.

Alib.

Well said; in a readiness, Lollio?   205

Lol.

Yes, sir.

Alib.

Away then, and guide them in, Lollio;
Entreat your mistress to see this sight.   [*Exit* LOLLIO.]
Hark, is there not one incurable fool
That might be begg'd? I have friends.   210

Lol.   [*within.*]

I have him for you—one that shall deserve it, too.

Alib.

Good boy, Lollio.
[*Reenter* ISABELLA, *then* LOLLIO *with Madmen and Fools.*]
                    The Madmen and Fools dance.
'Tis perfect; well, fit but once these strains,
We shall have coin and credit for our pains.   *Exeunt.*

---

204. *He . . . feather*] Franciscus seems to imagine praise of
his dancing.

210. *begg'd*] Have his estate turned over to me as guardian
(Schelling).

       friends] Presumably judges who could further his scheme.

213. *fit . . . strains*] Adjust my music to their dancing. Cf.
IV.iii.69.

ACTUS QUINTUS

[V.i]

Enter BEATRICE. *A clock strikes one.*

Bea.

One struck, and yet she lies by't! O, my fears!
This strumpet serves her own ends, 'tis apparent now;
Devours the pleasure with a greedy appetite
And never minds my honor or my peace;
Makes havoc of my right. But she pays dearly for't: 5
No trusting of her life with such a secret
That cannot rule her blood to keep her promise.
Beside, I have some suspicion of her faith to me,
Because I was suspected of my lord
And it must come from her.   *Strike two.*   10
                                   Hark, by my horrors,
Another clock strikes two.

Enter DE FLORES.

De F.   Pist! Where are you?

Bea.

De Flores?

V.i.] A Gallery in the Castle.
1. *lies by't*] Stays in Alsemero's bed.
5. *pays*] Shall pay.
6. *of her life*] Her alive.

115

De F.   Ay. Is she not come from him yet?
Bea.

As I am a living soul, not.
De F.   Sure, the devil
Hath sow'd his itch within her! Who'd trust
A waiting woman?
Bea.   I must trust somebody.   15
De F.

Push! They are termagants.
Especially when they fall upon their masters
And have their ladies' first fruits, th'are mad whelps;
You cannot stave 'em off from game royal. Then
You are so harsh and hardy, ask no counsel—   20
And I could have help'd you to an apothecary's daughter
Would have fall'n off before eleven, and thank'd you, too.
Bea.

O, me, not yet? This whore forgets herself.
De F.

The rascal fares so well. Look, y'are undone:
The daystar, by this hand! See Phosphorus plain yonder.   25
Bea.

Advise me now to fall upon some ruin;
There is no counsel safe, else.
De F.   Peace! I ha't now,
For we must force a rising; there's no remedy.

---

16. *termagants*] Violent women, hence presumably lustful.
17. *fall upon*] Happen to be taken to bed by.
19. *Then*] Moreover.
20. *harsh and hardy*] "Rough and tough," over-bold (in engaging Diaphanta without consulting De Flores).
22. *Would*] Who would.
        fall'n off] Withdrawn.
26. *to fall . . . ruin*] How to hit upon some spectacular disturbance.
28. *force a rising*] Get everybody out of bed.

Bea.

How? Take heed of that.

De F.   Tush! Be you quiet

Or else give over all.

Bea.   Prithee, I ha' done, then.   30

De F.

This is my reach: I'll set some part afire

Of Diaphanta's chamber.

Bea.   How? Fire, sir?

That may endanger the whole house.

De F.

You talk of danger when your fame's on fire.

Bea.

That's true. Do what thou wilt now.

De F.   Push! I aim   35

At a most rich success strikes all dead sure.

The chimney being afire, and some light parcels

Of the least danger in her chamber only,

If Diaphanta should be met by chance then,

Far from her lodging—which is now suspicious—   40

It would be thought her fears and affrights then

Drove her to seek for succor; if not seen

Or met at all—as that's the likeliest—

For her own shame she'll hasten towards her lodging.

I will be ready with a piece high-charg'd,   45

---

31. *reach*] Scheme.

34. *fame*] Reputation.

36. *success . . . sure*] Outcome that will surely take care of everything.

37–8. *and . . . only*] And some inflammable but harmless bundles being afire in her room, nowhere else.

40. *which . . . suspicious*] Which as things stand now would arouse suspicion.

45. *piece high-charg'd*] Heavily loaded musket.

As 'twere to cleanse the chimney; there 'tis proper now
But she shall be the mark.

Bea.   I'm forc'd to love thee now
'Cause thou provid'st so carefully for my honor.

De F.
'Slid, it concerns the safety of us both,
Our pleasure and continuance.

Bea.   One word, now, prithee: 50
How for the servants?

De F.   I'll despatch them,
Some one way, some another in the hurry,
For buckets, hooks, ladders; fear not you;
The deed shall find its time. And I've thought since
Upon a safe conveyance for the body, too.   55
How this fire purifies wit! Watch you your minute.

Bea.
Fear keeps my soul upon 't; I cannot stray from 't.

                    Enter ALONZO'S *Ghost.*

De F.
Ha! What art thou that tak'st away the light
'Twixt that star and me? I dread thee not;
'Twas but a mist of conscience.—All's clear again. *Exit.*   60

Bea.
Who's that, De Flores? Bless me! It slides by;

                                        [*Exit Ghost.*]

Some ill thing haunts the house; 't has left behind it
A shivering sweat upon me; I'm afraid now.

---

46. *As . . . chimney*] A crude but effective method of clear-
ing soot from a flue and thus putting out a chimney fire was to
discharge a gun up through it.

          there . . . now] In her room, where a chimney is sup-
posed to be on fire, a musket will be understandable.

49. *'Slid*] By God's eyelid; a mild oath.

50. *Our . . . continuance*] Our sexual enjoyment and its
continuance.

This night hath been so tedious! O, this strumpet!
Had she a thousand lives, he should not leave her   65
Till he had destroy'd the last. List! O, my terrors!
Three struck by Saint Sebastian's! *Struck three o'clock.*

Within.   Fire, fire, fire!

Bea.

Already? How rare is that man's speed!
How heartily he serves me! His face loathes one,   70
But look upon his care, who would not love him?
The East is not more beauteous than his service.

Within.

Fire, fire, fire!

  Reenter DE FLORES. *Servants pass over, ring a bell.*

De F.

Away, despatch! Hooks, buckets, ladders; that's well said:
The firebell rings, the chimney works. My charge!   75
The piece is ready.   *Exit.*

Bea.   Here's a man worth loving—

   Enter DIAPHANTA.

O, y'are a jewel!

Dia.   Pardon frailty, madam.
In troth I was so well I ev'n forgot myself.

Bea.

Y'have made trim work.

Dia.   What?

Bea.   Hie quickly to your chamber;
Your reward follows you.

Dia.   I never made   80
So sweet a bargain.   *Exit.*

---

64. *tedious*] Vexatious.
65. *he*] De Flores.
70. *heartily*] Faithfully.
 loathes one] Makes one loathe it.
75. *works*] Burns.
80. *reward*] 1) The thousand ducats; 2) death.

Enter ALSEMERO.

Als.   O, my dear Joanna,
Alas, art thou risen, too? I was coming,
My absolute treasure!
Bea.   When I miss'd you
I could not choose but follow.
Als.   Th'art all sweetness.—
The fire is not so dangerous.
Bea.   Think you so, sir?   85
Als.
I prithee, tremble not. Believe me, 'tis not.
        Enter VERMANDERO, JASPERINO.
Ver.
O, bless my house and me!
Als.   My lord your father.
        Enter DE FLORES *with a piece.*
Ver.
Knave, whither goes that piece?
De F.   To scour the chimney.   *Exit.*
Ver.
O, well said, well said!
That fellow's good on all occasions.   90
Bea.
A wondrous necessary man, my lord.
Ver.
He hath a ready wit; he's worth 'em all, sir:
Dog at a house of fire; I ha' seen him sing'd ere now—
                              The piece goes off.
Ha, there he goes.
Bea.   [*aside.*]
        'Tis done.

82–4.] Since Diaphanta enters (l. 76.1) before Alsemero
(l. 81.1), Beatrice cannot be sure which of them rose first.
Alsemero's greeting gives her her cue.

93. *Dog . . . fire*] An efficient firefighter.

Als.   Come, sweet, to bed now;
    Alas, thou wilt get cold.
Bea.   The fear keeps that out: 95
    My heart will find no quiet till I hear
    How Diaphanta, my poor woman, fares;
    It is her chamber, sir, her lodging chamber.
Ver.
    How should the fire come there?
Bea.
    As good a soul as ever lady countenanc'd,   100
    But in her chamber negligent and heavy.
    She scap'd a mine twice.
Ver.   Twice?
Bea.   Strangely twice, sir.
Ver.
    Those sleepy sluts are dangerous in a house,
    An they be ne'er so good.
                    Enter DE FLORES.
De F.   O, poor virginity!
    Thou hast paid dearly for't.
Ver.   Bless us! What's that?   105
De F.
    A thing you all knew once. Diaphanta's burnt.
Bea.
    My woman, O, my woman!
De F.   Now the flames
    Are greedy of her; burnt, burnt, burnt to death, sir.
Bea.
    O, my presaging soul!

---

100. *countenanc'd*] Sponsored.
101. *heavy*] Clumsy.
102. *mine*] A buried or submerged explosive; hence, any
danger difficult to detect and avoid. Perhaps Beatrice is thinking
of the chastity test and the bed-switching.
104. *An*] Here, "though" rather than "if."

Als.   Not a tear more!
I charge you by the last embrace I gave you   110
In bed before this rais'd us.
Bea.   Now you tie me;
Were it my sister, now she gets no more.
Enter Servant.
Ver.
How now?
Ser.
All danger's past; you may now take your rests, my
lords; the fire is throughly quench'd. Ah, poor gentle-   115
woman, how soon was she stifled!
Bea.
De Flores, what is left of her inter,
And we as mourners all will follow her:
I will entreat that honor to my servant
Ev'n of my lord himself.
Als.   Command it, sweetness.   120
Bea.
Which of you spied the fire first?
De F.   'Twas I, madam.
Bea.
And took such pains in't, too? A double goodness!
'Twere well he were rewarded.
Ver.   He shall be;
De Flores, call upon me.
Als.   And upon me, sir.
Exeunt.   [*Manet* DE FLORES.]
De F.
Rewarded? Precious! Here's a trick beyond me;   125

---

111. *tie*] Bind. Beatrice is playing the obedient wife.
115. *throughly*] Thoroughly.
116. *stifled*] Suffocated. De Flores (l. 106, above) says *burnt*.
125. *Precious*] "Priceless!"

I see in all bouts, both of sport and wit,
Always a woman strives for the last hit.   *Exit.*

[V.ii]
Enter TOMAZO.

Tom.
  I cannot taste the benefits of life
  With the same relish I was wont to do.
  Man I grow weary of, and hold his fellowship
  A treacherous, bloody friendship; and because
  I am ignorant in whom my wrath should settle   5
  I must think all men villains, and the next
  I meet, whoe'er he be, the murderer
  Of my most worthy brother. Ha! What's he?
Enter DE FLORES, *passes over the stage.*
  O, the fellow that some call honest De Flores;
  But methinks honesty was hard bestead   10
  To come there for a lodging: as if a queen
  Should make her palace of a pesthouse.
  I find a contrariety in nature
  Betwixt that face and me; the least occasion
  Would give me game upon him; yet he's so foul   15
  One would scarce touch [him] with a sword he loved
  And made account of; so most deadly venomous
  He would go near to poison any weapon
  That should draw blood on him; one must resolve
  Never to use that sword again in fight,   20
  In way of honest manhood, that strikes him;

V.ii.] An Apartment in the Castle.
10. *hard bestead*] "Hard up."
13. *contrariety in nature*] Instinctive enmity. See l. 40, below.
14–15. *the . . . him*] I'd (fight and) beat him on the slightest
provocation.
16. *one . . . he*] One . . . one.

Some river must devour't, 'twere not fit
That any man should find it. What, again?
                    Reenter DE FLORES.
He walks a purpose by, sure, to choke me up,
To infect my blood.
De F.   My worthy, noble lord!   25
Tom.
Dost offer to come near and breathe upon me?
                                        [*Strikes him.*]
De F.
A blow!   [*Draws his sword.*]
Tom.   Yea, are you so prepar'd?
I'll rather like a soldier die by th' sword
Than like a politician by thy poison.   [*Draws.*]
De F.
Hold, my lord, as you are honorable.   30
Tom.
All slaves that kill by poison are still cowards.
De F.   [*aside.*]
I cannot strike; I see his brother's wounds
Fresh bleeding in his eye, as in a crystal.—
I will not question this; I know y'are noble;
I take my injury with thanks given, sir,   35
Like a wise lawyer; and as a favor
Will wear it for the worthy hand that gave it.
[*Aside.*] Why this from him, that yesterday appear'd
So strangely loving to me?

---

24. *a*] On.
    choke me up] With loathing.
29. *like a politician*] Pretending friendship.
31. *cowards*] Because De Flores does not fight.
33. *fresh bleeding*] Perhaps an allusion to the old belief that
the victim's wounds bled afresh in the murderer's presence.
    as in a crystal] Perfectly clearly.
36. *like . . . lawyer*] Cf. l. 29n., above.

O, but instinct is of a subtler strain: 40
Guilt must not walk so near his lodge again;
He came near me now.   *Exit.*

Tom.

All league with mankind I renounce forever
Till I find this murderer; not so much
As common courtesy but I'll lock up;   45
For in the state of ignorance I live in
A brother may salute his brother's murderer
And wish good speed to th' villain in a greeting.
            Enter VERMANDERO, ALIBIUS, *and* ISABELLA.

Ver.

Noble Piracquo!

Tom.   Pray keep on your way, sir,
I've nothing to say to you.

Ver.   Comforts bless you, sir.   50

Tom.

I have forsworn compliment, in troth I have, sir;
As you are merely man, I have not left
A good wish for you nor any here.

Ver.

Unless you be so far in love with grief
You will not part from't upon any terms,   55
We bring that news will make a welcome for us.

Tom.

What news can that be?

Ver.   Throw no scornful smile
Upon the zeal I bring you; 'tis worth more, sir.

---

41. *his lodge*] Its lodge, that of instinct.
42.] He was very near to sensing my guilt just now.
51. *compliment*] Formal courtesy.
52. *As . . . man*] See l. 43, above.
    merely] Nothing but.
55. *You*] That you.
56. *will*] That will.

Two of the chiefest men I kept about me
I hide not from the law, or your just vengeance.   60
Tom.
    Ha!
Ver.
To give your peace more ample satisfaction,
Thank these discoverers.
Tom.   If you bring that calm,
Name but the manner I shall ask forgiveness in
For that contemptuous smile upon you;   65
I'll perfect it with reverence that belongs
Unto a sacred altar.   [*Kneels.*]
Ver.   Good sir, rise;   [*Raising him.*]
Why, now you overdo as much a this hand
As you fell short a t'other.—Speak, Alibius.
Alib.
'Twas my wife's fortune—as she is most lucky   70
At a discovery—to find out lately
Within our hospital of fools and madmen
Two counterfeits slipp'd into these disguises;
Their names, Franciscus and Antonio.
Ver.
Both mine, sir, and I ask no favor for 'em.   75
Alib.
Now, that which draws suspicion to their habits:
The time of their disguisings agrees justly
With the day of the murder.
Tom.   O, blest revelation!
Ver.
Nay more, nay more, sir—I'll not spare mine own

---

63. *discoverers*] Informants, Alibius and Isabella.
68–9. *a . . . a*] On . . . on.
75. *favor*] Leniency.
76. *habits*] Costumes, disguises.

In way of justice—they both feign'd a journey   80
To Briamata, and so wrought out their leaves;
My love was so abus'd in't.
Tom.   Time's too precious
To run in waste now; you have brought a peace
The riches of five kingdoms could not purchase.
Be my most happy conduct; I thirst for 'em;   85
Like subtle lightning will I wind about 'em
And melt their marrow in 'em.   *Exeunt.*

[V.iii]

Enter ALSEMERO *and* JASPERINO.

Jas.

Your confidence, I'm sure, is now of proof.
The prospect from the garden has show'd
Enough for deep suspicion.
Als.   The black mask
That so continually was worn upon't
Condemns the face for ugly ere't be seen: 5
Her despite to him, and so seeming-bottomless.
Jas.

Touch it home, then: 'tis not a shallow probe

80–1. *they . . . Briamata*] Cf. IV.ii.7–8. Such inaccuracies
are unimportant in the theater.

81. *wrought out*] "Worked me for."

85. *conduct*] Here, guide.

    thirst] Cf. II.ii.133 (Bawcutt).

V.iii.] Alsemero's Apartment in the Castle.

1. *of proof*] Impenetrable as armor.

3. *black mask*] Beatrice's seeming-bottomless loathing of De
Flores. Cf. ll. 6, 46–7.

5. *face*] Their true relationship.

7. *Touch*] Probe.

    it] The whole corrupt matter.

    home] To the quick.

Can search this ulcer soundly; I fear you'll find it
Full of corruption. 'Tis fit I leave you:
She meets you opportunely from that walk;   10
She took the back door at his parting with her.
                                        Exit JASPERINO.

Als.

Did my fate wait for this unhappy stroke
At my first sight of woman? She's here!
                        Enter BEATRICE.

Bea.

Alsemero!

Als.   How do you?

Bea.   How do I?

Alas! How do you? You look not well.   15

Als.

You read me well enough: I am not well.

Bea.

Not well, sir? Is't in my power to better you?

Als.

Yes.

Bea.   Nay, then y'are cur'd again.

Als.

Pray resolve me one question, lady.

Bea.   If I can.

Als.

None can so sure. Are you honest?   20

Bea.

Ha, ha, ha! That's a broad question, my lord.

Als.

But that's not a modest answer, my lady.
Do you laugh? My doubts are strong upon me.

Bea.

'Tis innocence that smiles, and no rough brow

---

19. *resolve me*] Decide.
20. *honest*] A faithful wife.

Can take away the dimple in her cheek.   25
Say I should strain a tear to fill the vault,
Which would you give the better faith to?

Als.

'Twere but hypocrisy of a sadder color
But the same stuff; neither your smiles nor tears
Shall move or flatter me from my belief: 30
You are a whore!

Bea.   What a horrid sound it hath!
It blasts a beauty to deformity;
Upon what face soever that breath falls,
It strikes it ugly. O, you have ruin'd
What you can ne'er repair again.   35

Als.

I'll all demolish and seek out truth within you
If there be any left. Let your sweet tongue
Prevent your heart's rifling; there I'll ransack
And tear out my suspicion.

Bea.   You may, sir;
'Tis an easy passage; yet, if you please,   40
Show me the ground whereon you lost your love.
My spotless virtue may but tread on that
Before I perish.

Als.   Unanswerable;
A ground you cannot stand on. You fall down
Beneath all grace and goodness when you set   45
Your ticklish heel on't. There was a visor

---

26. *tear . . . vault*] A tear that would fill the vault of heaven.

28. *sadder color*] 1) Darker hue; 2) pretence to cover a graver fault.

38. *ransack*] Search without pity.

43. *Unanswerable*] On a ground (l. 41) you can't explain away.

46. *ticklish*] Wanton.

  visor] Cf. l. 3, above.

O'er that cunning face, and that became you;
Now impudence in triumph rides upon't.
How comes this tender reconcilement, else,
'Twixt you and your despite, your rancorous loathing,   50
De Flores? He that your eye was sore at sight of,
He's now become your arm's supporter, your
Lips' saint.

Bea.   Is there the cause?

Als.   Worse: your lust's devil,
Your adultery!

Bea.   Would any but yourself say that,
'Twould turn him to a villain.

Als.   'Twas witness'd   55
By the counsel of your bosom, Diaphanta.

Bea.
Is your witness dead, then?

Als.   'Tis to be fear'd
It was the wages of her knowledge; poor soul,
She liv'd not long after the discovery.

Bea.
Then hear a story of not much less horror   60
Than this your false suspicion is beguil'd with.
To your bed's scandal I stand up innocence,
Which even the guilt of one black other deed
Will stand for proof of: your love has made me
A cruel murd'ress.

---

48. *impudence*] Shamelessness.

50. *despite*] Object of loathing.

53. *cause*] Cf. 1. 41, above.

53–4. *your . . . adultery*] He's now become (1. 52) your
devil of lust, your partner in adultery. *OED* does not list this
meaning under *adultery*.

58. *It*] Her death.

62. *To . . . innocence*] To the charge of having brought
scandal upon your bed, I set up the plea of innocence.

Als.   Ha!

Bea.   A bloody one.   65
I have kiss'd poison for't, strok'd a serpent;
That thing of hate, worthy in my esteem
Of no better employment, and him most worthy
To be so employ'd, I caus'd to murder
That innocent Piracquo, having no   70
Better means than that worst, to assure
Yourself to me.

Als.   O, the place itself e'er since
Has crying been for vengeance: the temple
Where blood and beauty first unlawfully
Fir'd their devotion and quench'd the right one!   75
'Twas in my fears at first, 'twill have it now.
O, thou art all deform'd!

Bea.   Forget not, sir,
It for your sake was done. Shall greater dangers
Make the less welcome?

Als.   O, thou shouldst have gone
A thousand leagues about to have avoided   80
This dangerous bridge of blood. Here we are lost.

Bea.
Remember I am true unto your bed.

Als.
The bed itself's a charnel, the sheets shrouds
For murdered carcasses. It must ask pause

---

66. *poison . . . serpent*] De Flores.

75. *right one*] Devotion to God.

77. *deform'd*] Changed from beauty to ugliness. Cf. ll. 197–8,
below.

78–9. *shall . . . welcome*] Shall the greater dangers I have
dared for you make my welcome the less?

80. *about*] Out of your way.

81. *bridge of blood*] Bloody means of bridging the chasm
between us, your betrothal to Alonzo.

What I must do in this; meantime you shall   85
Be my prisoner only. Enter my closet;   *Exit* BEATRICE.
I'll be your keeper yet. O, in what part
Of this sad story shall I first begin? Ha!

Enter DE FLORES.

This same fellow has put me in. De Flores!
De F.
Noble Alsemero?
Als.   I can tell you   90
News, sir: my wife has her commended to you.
De F.
That's news indeed, my lord; I think she would
Commend me to the gallows if she could,
She ever lov'd me so well, I thank her.
Als.
What's this blood upon your band, De Flores?   95
De F.
Blood? No, sure, 'twas wash'd since.
Als.   Since when, man?
De F.
Since t'other day I got a knock
In a sword and dagger school; I think 'tis out.
Als.
Yes, 'tis almost out, but 'tis perceiv'd, though.
I had forgot my message; this it is: 100
What price goes murder?
De F.   How, sir?
Als.   I ask you, sir.
My wife's behindhand with you, she tells me,

---

87. *yet*] For the time being.
89. *put me in*] Given me my cue (Schelling).
95. *band*] Cuff.
98. *out*] Washed out, invisible.
102. *behindhand with*] Indebted to.

For a brave, bloody blow you gave for her sake
Upon Piracquo.

De F.   [*aside.*]
        Upon? 'Twas quite through him, sure.—
Has she confess'd it?

Als.   As sure as death to both of you,   105
And much more than that.

De F.   It could not be much more;
'Twas but one thing, and that: she's a whore.

Als.

It could not choose but follow. O, cunning devils!
How should blind men know you from fair-fac'd saints?

Bea. within.

He lies! The villain does belie me!   110

De F.

Let me go to her, sir.

Als.   Nay, you shall to her.—
Peace, crying crocodile, your sounds are heard.
Take your prey to you.—Get you in to her, sir.
                      Exit DE FLORES.
I'll be your pander now; rehearse again
Your scene of lust, that you may be perfèct   115
When you shall come to act it to the black audience
Where howls and gnashings shall be music to you.—
Clip your adult'ress freely; 'tis the pilot
Will guide you to the Mare Mortuum,

---

103. *brave*] Fine.

112. *crocodile*] Believed to weep while devouring its prey.

113. *your prey*] De Flores, who *is* her victim in a way.

115. *perfèct*] Perfected in your roles.

118. *clip*] Embrace.
     'tis the pilot] She's the pilot who.

119. *Mare Mortuum*] The Sea of the Dead. In Homer and later Greek poets the entrance to Hades was across the ocean or beside deep lakes.

Where you shall sink to fathoms bottomless.   120

Enter VERMANDERO, ALIBIUS, ISABELLA, TOMAZO,
FRANCISCUS, *and* ANTONIO.

Ver.

O, Alsemero, I have a wonder for you.

Als.

No, sir, 'tis I; I have a wonder for you.

Ver.

I have suspicion near as proof itself
For Piracquo's murder.

Als.   Sir, I have proof
Beyond suspicion for Piracquo's murder.   125

Ver.

Beseech you hear me: these two have been disguis'd
E'er since the deed was done.

Als.   I have two other
That were more close disguis'd than your two could be,
E'er since the deed was done.

Ver.

You'll hear me! These mine own servants—   130

Als.

Hear me those nearer than your servants,
That shall acquit them and prove them guiltless.

Fran.

That may be done with easy truth, sir.

Tom.

How is my cause bandied through your delays!
'Tis urgent in blood and calls for haste.   135
Give me a brother alive or dead;
Alive, a wife with him; if dead, for both

---

128. *close*] Impenetrably.

131. *me*] Ethical dative: "because I ask it."

132. *That*] Who.

135. *in blood*] Because I am his brother.

A recompense: for murder and adultery.
Bea. within.
O, O, O!
Als.   Hark! 'Tis coming to you.
De F. within.
Nay, I'll along for company.
Bea. within.   O, O!   140
Ver.
What horrid sounds are these?
Als.
Come forth, you twins of mischief!
    Enter DE FLORES *bringing in* BEATRICE [*wounded*].
De F.
Here we are; if you have any more
To say to us, speak quickly; I shall not
Give you the hearing, else; I am so stout yet,   145
And so, I think, that broken rib of mankind.
Ver.
An host of enemies ent'red my citadel
Could not amaze like this! Joanna! Beatrice-Joanna!
Bea.
O, come not near me, sir, I shall defile you.
I am that of your blood was taken from you   150

---

138. *recompense*] Retribution.

    adultery] Tomazo may have regarded her marriage to Alsemero as adulterous and betrothal to Alonzo still valid.

    139. *O*] De Flores has wounded Beatrice. See l. 142.1, below.

    'Tis] Your recompense is.

    140. *I'll . . . company*] De Flores means to kill himself. See ll. 144–5, below.

    145. *so stout yet*] Still strong enough.

    150–4. *I . . . stars*] I am the evil in your blood that was let to make you well. Behold it no more, but throw it to the ground uncaring. Let the common sewer swallow its identity, so that the stars themselves no longer behold it.

For your better health. Look no more upon't,
But cast it to the ground regardlessly;
Let the common sewer take it from distinction
Beneath the stars. Upon yon meteor
Ever hung my fate, 'mongst things corruptible;   155
I ne'er could pluck it from him; my loathing
Was prophet to the rest, but ne'er believ'd;
Mine honor fell with him, and now my life.—
Alsemero, I am a stranger to your bed;
Your bed was coz'ned on the nuptial night,   160
For which your false bride died.

Als.   Diaphanta!

De F.

Yes; and the while I coupled with your mate
At barley-break; now we are left in hell.

Ver.

We are all there; it circumscribes here.

De F.

I lov'd this woman in spite of her heart;   165
Her love I earn'd out of Piracquo's murder.

Tom.

Ha! My brother's murderer!

De F.   Yes; and her honor's prize
Was my reward. I thank life for nothing

---

153. *sewer*] The Q reading *shewer,* shore, is very tempting, especially with *ground* (l. 153). The common shore was the no-man's-land by the waterside, where filth was deposited for the tide to wash away.

154. *yon meteor*] Yonder evil, earth-bound shooting star, De Flores.

161. *For which*] For her part in which deception.

162–3. *coupled . . . barley-break*] As often, committed adultery. See III.iii.165n., and l. 119, above.

       it . . . here] Hell encompasses this place.

165. *her heart*] Which loved another and loathed me.

But that pleasure; it was so sweet to me
That I have drunk up all, left none behind   170
For any man to pledge me.

Ver.   Horrid villain!
Keep life in him for further tortures.

De F.   No!
I can prevent you: here's my penknife still.
It is but one thread more [*stabs himself*] and now 'tis cut.
Make haste, Joanna, by that token to thee: 175
Canst not forget, so lately put in mind,
I would not go to leave thee far behind.   *Dies.*

Bea.
Forgive me, Alsemero, all forgive!
'Tis time to die when 'tis a shame to live.   *Dies.*

Ver.
O!   180
My name is ent'red now in that record
Where till this fatal hour 'twas never read.

Als.
Let it be blotted out; let your heart lose it,
And it can never look you in the face
Nor tell a tale behind the back of life   185
To your dishonor; justice hath so right
The guilty hit that innocence is quit
By proclamation, and may joy again.
[*To* TOMAZO.] Sir, you are sensible of what truth hath
    done;
'Tis the best comfort that your grief can find.   190

---

171. *pledge me*] Drink with me.

173. *prevent*] Get ahead of.

175. *token to thee*] Wound I gave you.

181. *record*] The book of heaven.

187–8. *quit By proclamation*] Cleared of suspicion by public
proclamation of the truth (Bawcutt).

Tom.

Sir, I am satisfied; my injuries
Lie dead before me. I can exact no more
Unless my soul were loose and could o'ertake
Those black fugitives that are fled from thence,
To take a second vengeance; but there are wraths   195
Deeper than mine, 'tis to be fear'd, about 'em.

Als.

What an opacous body had that moon
That last chang'd on us! Here's beauty chang'd
To ugly whoredom; here, servant obedience
To a master sin, imperious murder;   200
I, a suppos'd husband, chang'd embraces
With wantonness—but that was paid before.
[*To* TOMAZO.] Your change is come, too: from an
    ignorant wrath
To knowing friendship. Are there any more on's?

Ant.

Yes, sir; I was chang'd, too, from a little ass as I was   205
to a great fool as I am; and had like to ha' been
chang'd to the gallows but that, you know, my innocence always excuses me.

---

191. *injuries*] Wrongs, in the dead forms of Beatrice and De
Flores.

194. *black fugitives*] Their wicked souls.
    thence] From their bodies there.

196. *about 'em*] Punishing them.

197. *opacous*] Clouded, ominous.

200. *imperious*] All-conquering.

202.] With wanton Diaphanta—but she has been punished
already.

207. *innocence*] 1) Guiltlessness; 2) idiocy (Dyce).

Fran.

I was chang'd from a little wit to be stark mad,
Almost for the same purpose.

Isa.   [*to* ALIBIUS.]
                              Your change is still behind,   210
But deserve best your transformation.
You are a jealous coxcomb, keep schools of folly,
And teach your scholars how to break your own head.

Alib.

I see all apparent, wife, and will change now
Into a better husband, and never keep   215
Scholars that shall be wiser than myself.

Als.   [*to* VERMANDERO.]
Sir, you have yet a son's duty living;
Please you, accept it; let that your sorrow
As it goes from your eye go from your heart;
Man and his sorrow at the grave must part.   220

Epilogue.
[*Spoken by* ALSEMERO.]

All we can do to comfort one another,
To stay a brother's sorrow for a brother,
To dry a child from the kind father's eyes,
Is to no purpose: it rather multiplies.
Your only smiles have power to cause relive   225

---

210. *behind*] To come.

211. *deserve best*] Prove yourself best deserving of.

213. *break . . . head*] Put the cuckold's horns on your own forehead.

217. *son's duty living*] Respect and obedience of a living son.

218. *Let that*] Let.

224. *it*] Sorrow.

225. *Your only*] Only your.

The dead again, or in their rooms to give
Brother a new brother, father a child;
If these appear, all griefs are reconcil'd.

Exeunt omnes.

FINIS.

---

226. *rooms*] Places.
227. *Brother . . . brother*] Tomazo . . . Vermandero.
  father . . . child] Vermandero . . . Alsemero.
228. *These*] Your smiles.

APPENDIX

Substantive Emendations of Q in this Edition (see p. 11)

Dramatis personae 18 *Alicante*] *Allegant* Q

I.i.4 *of*] Ed.; *or* 50 aside] Ed. 56 aside] Ed. Q 57.1 Enter . . .
Servants.] Enter . . . Servants, Joanna. Q 57.2 They talk apart.]
Ed. 100 *Will't*] Dilke; *Wilt* Q 111 *of*] Dilke; *or* Q 128 *What*]
Dilke; *And what* Q 143 *ingredient*] *Ingredian* Q 149 kisses her]
Ed. 175 *Iulan*] Dyce; *Julan* Q 189 *his*] Schelling (Dyce conj.);
this Q 231 *come, . . . mischief! Now*] Ed.; *come; . . . mischief:*
Now Q 234 *here. I*] Ed.; *here I* Q 235–236 *Yet . . . matter: If*
. . . still:] Schelling; *Yet . . . her: No . . . still,* Q

I.ii.124 *you I*] Bawcutt; *you* Q 184 *stand there*] *stad thenre* Q
195 *the bread's*] Dyce; *he breades* Q

II.i.68 *wilt*] Dilke; *wil't* Q 68 Aside] Ed. 124 as a separate line]
Ed. 139–140 *him, . . . passions. And . . . dangerous*] Ed.; *him,*
. . . passions, and . . . dangerous Q 144 *an*] *and* Q 151 *w'are*]
corrected copies of Q; *we are* uncorrected copies

II.ii.7 *lock'd*] Dilke; *lock* Q 14 Kisses her.] Ed. 33 *y'are danger's*]
Dyce; *your dangers* Q 39 *ha' dried*] Dyce; *a-dried* Q 80 *Faugh*]
Dyce; *vauh* Q 131 *myself of that*] corrected copies of Q; *myselfe*
that uncorrected copies

141

III.iii.60 Rises] Ed. 69 *ago*—] Ed.; *agoe,* Q 70 *might*—] Ed.; *might.* Q 88 *him now,*] Ed.; *him, now* Q 134 *he*] Dyce; *she* Q. 135 *the nearest*] Dilke; *nearest* Q 137 *withal! Certain, you*] Dilke; *withall certain: You* Q

III.iv.18 *banquet; for* . . . *deed;*] Dyce; *banquet for* . . . *deed,* Q 70 *have [slept at ease]*] Dilke; *have,* Q112 *it not*] Dilke; *it* Q 163 *may you*] Dyce; *may* Q

IV.i.5 *that's*] Bawcutt; *both* Q 24 *Experiment*] *Experimen [n* broken, resembling *r.*] Q 29 *down*] Dilke; *dow* Q 89 *aside*] Ed. 98 *hear't; then*] Schelling; *hear't then,* Q

IV.ii.54 *chins and noses*] Ellis (Dyce conj.); *sins and vices* Q 60 *'Twill*] Dilke; *I will* Q 60, 60.1, 61 *reckon.* Enter ALSEMERO. *Sir!*] Dyce; *reckon sir.* Enter Alsemero. Q 61–62 *Sir! You* . . . *back;*] Schelling; one line Dyce 89 *though*] Dilke; *thou* Q 117 *since,*] *since?* Q 132 *'Tis*] Dilke; *'T's* Q 141 *qualitied?*] Dilke; *qualited.* Q 149 *Keeps*] Dyce; *Keep* Q

IV.iii.2 *at once*] Dyce; *once* Q 6.1 Gives . . . *letter.*] Ed. 34 *you, mistress*] *your mistress* some copies of Q (Lawrence) 44 *Why,*] Dilke; *We* Q 46 *Ab-use*] Ed.; *Abuse* Q 92 *an*] *and* Q 98 *rises*] Dilke; *rise* Q 102 *he*] Dilke; *she* Q 102 *Shoo*] *Shough* Q 116 *straits*] Dyce; *streets* Q 130 Reveals herself.] Ed. 138 *fool*—] Schelling; *fool?* Q 157–159 prose] Ed. 162 *cast off*] Dyce; *cast* Q 166 *which have*] Dyce; *which* Q 172 *What do*] Dilke; *What? Do* Q 178 *Stay*] *tay* Q 208 Exit LOLLIO.] Ed. 211 Within.] Ed. 213 *perfect; well, fit*] Dyce; *perfect well fit,* Q

V.i.21 *an*] Dilke; *a* Q 22 *thank'd*] Dilke; *thank* Q 25 *Phosphorus*] Dilke; *Bosphorus* Q 95 *The fear*] Ed.; *Alas, the fear* Q 104 *An*] *And* Q

V.ii.16 *touch him*] Dilke; *touch* Q 18 *near*] Dyce; *ne're* Q 42 *near*] Dyce; *ne're* Q 81 *Briamata*] Dyce; *Bramata* Q

V.iii.61 *with.*] Ed.; *with,* Q 107 *that:*] Ed.; *that* Q 108 *It*] Dilke;
I Q 153 *sewer*] Dilke; *shewer* Q 155 *hung*] Dyce; *hang* Q 180
as a separate line] Ed.